The E-MYTH Physician

WHY MOST MEDICAL
PRACTICES DON'T WORK
AND WHAT TO DO ABOUT IT

MICHAEL E. GERBER

HarperBusiness
An Imprint of HarperCollins*Publishers*

HarperCollins books may be purchased for educational, business, or sales promotional use. For information please write: Special Markets Department, HarperCollins Publishers Inc., 10 East 53rd Street, New York, NY 10022.

FIRST EDITION

DESIGNED BY MARY AUSTIN SPEAKER

Printed on acid-free paper

Library of Congress Cataloging-in-Publication Data

Gerber, Michael E.
    The E-myth physician : why most medical practices don't work and what to do about it / Michael E. Gerber.
        p. cm.
    ISBN 0-06-621469-6
        1. Medicine—Practice—Finance. I. Title.
    R728.G37 2003
    610'.681'1—dc21   2002068853

05   06   07   RRD/   10   9   8   7   6   5   4

The basic difference between an ordinary man
and a warrior is that a warrior takes everything
as a challenge while an ordinary man takes
everything either as a blessing or a curse.

DON JUAN IN *TALES OF POWER*
CARLOS CASTANEDA

Whenever anything is being accomplished,
it is being done . . . by a monomaniac with a mission.

P. DRUCKER, QUOTED IN
RIPPLES FROM THE ZAMBESI, BY ERNESTO SIROLLI

CONTENTS

PREFACE

I am not a Doctor, though I have helped dozens of Doctors reinvent their medical practices over the past 25 years.

I've learned there are two kinds of Doctors. In the first category are Doctors who own their practice. They're slogging through each day, putting out fires, trying to support their family. Although these Doctors often have cloudy vision, they are in fact visionaries. In the second category are Doctors who lack or have abandoned such vision. They work for the HMOs and the insurance companies. This book will have its greatest appeal to the first group.

Most medical practices today are failing—not necessarily going out of business (though many are doing that every day) but failing to fulfill the potential the Doctor envisioned in those halcyon days of medical school. Most Doctors who own their own practice don't own a true business but a job . . . doing it, doing it, doing it . . . hoping like hell to get some time off, but never figuring out how to get their practice to run without them. That's where E-Myth comes in.

I like to view myself as a thinker, even a dreamer. Yes, I like to *do* things, but before I jump into a project, I like to think it through and figure out the best way to do it. I try to see the finished product in my mind's eye. I imagine the impossible, then try to figure out how the impossible can become the possible. And how the possible can become reality.

Over the years, I've made it my business to study how things work and how people work—specifically, how things and people work best together to produce optimum results, and how to create an organization that can do great things and achieve results better than any other organization.

The end product has been a series of books I've authored—*The E-Myth* books—as well as a company, E-Myth Worldwide, which I founded in 1977. E-Myth Worldwide has helped thousands of small business owners—including many Doctors—reinvent the way they do business by (1) rethinking the purpose of their business and (2) imagining how it could fulfill that purpose in innovative ways.

This book is about how to produce the best results as a real-world Doctor in the development, expansion, and liberation of your medical company. In the process, you will come to understand what the practice of medicine—as a *business*—is and what it isn't.

Although this book is small, it's about big ideas that may at first overwhelm you. That's not because I'm so smart, but rather because the way most Doctors run their practice is light-years away from the recommendations in this book.

My aim is to help you begin the exciting process of transforming the way you do business as a medical practitioner. As such, I'm confident that *The E-Myth Physician* could well be the most important book on the practice of medicine as a business you'll ever read.

Unlike other books on this subject, I don't try to tell you how to do your work as a Doctor; you already know how to do that. Rather, I strive to offer insights into how great businesspeople think, whether they are Doctors or not.

Most Doctors don't think of themselves as businesspeople—and that's the problem. Because that's exactly what they have to be to own a practice. In fact, most practices fail to fulfill their potential not because of the Doctor's medical skills, or because of what's going on outside the medical practice, such as managed care, defiant insurers, and increased costs. Rather they fail because Doctors are not prepared for what is about to happen to them. They are simply unprepared for the business of medicine. Victims of an "entrepreneurial seizure," they believe that because they understand how to do the technical work—the work of a Doctor—they understand how to build a successful business that does that work.

The truth is that learning how to be a Doctor does not prepare you to develop a successful medical practice. Knowing how a practice works best has little to do with knowing how a Doctor works best.

In fact, it's the chasm between being a Doctor and an entrepreneur (a true businessperson) that is the primary cause of the malaise, disaffection, and frustration experienced by most Doctors who own their own practice.

No matter how much the Doctor knows about the work of doctoring, none of that expertise is in itself sufficient to build a successful practice, business, or enterprise. It's only the beginning.

The good news, Doctor, is that you can avoid these pitfalls. Despite what you may think about patients, insurance companies, and HMOs trying to destroy your practice, the E-Myth philosophy, when applied to your practice, will transform it into a flourishing business and an extraordinary enterprise—to the degree you want it to.

I'm convinced that although the E-Myth philosophy is a new way of thinking for most Doctors, they must adopt it if their practice is to flourish. I call this new perspective Strategic Thinking, as opposed to Tactical Thinking.

In Strategic Thinking, also called Systems Thinking, you, the Doctor, will begin to think about your entire practice—the broad scope of it—instead of just its individual parts. You will begin to see the End Game (perhaps for the first time) rather than just the day-to-day routine in which you and your employees are continually immersed—the work I call *doing it, doing it, doing it.*

Understanding Strategic Thinking will enable you to create a practice that becomes a successful business, with the potential to flourish as an even more successful enterprise. But in order for you to accomplish this, your practice, your business, and certainly your enterprise must work *apart* from you instead of *because* of you.

The E-Myth philosophy says that a highly successful medical practice can grow into a highly successful medical *business,* which in turn can become the foundation for an inordinately successful medical *enterprise* that works *apart* from the Doctor-owner instead of *because* of the Doctor-owner.

According to the E-Myth, the key to transforming your practice—and your life—is to grasp the profound difference between going to work *on* your practice (Systems Thinker) and going to work *in* your practice (Tactical Thinker). It's the difference between going to work on your practice as an entrepreneur and going to work in your practice as a Doctor.

The two are not mutually exclusive. In fact, they are essential to each other. The problem with most medical practices is that the Systems Thinker—the entrepreneur—is completely absent. And so is the vision.

The E-Myth says that the key to transforming

your practice into a successful enterprise is knowing how to transform yourself from successful medical technician (Doctor) to successful medical technician-manager-entrepreneur.

In the process, everything you do in your practice will be transformed. The door is then open to turning it into the kind of practice it should be—a practice, a business, an enterprise of pure joy!

In E-Myth terminology, the business you're going to create is called NewCo, whereas OldCo is the business you have. This book aims to help you invent NewCo. Think of NewCo as starting all over. Ask these questions: If I were beginning again in medicine, what would I do differently? What would NewCo look like, feel like, be like? It's all about seeing your medical company as though for the first time.

Is your medical company a practice, a business, or an enterprise? By the time you finish this book, you'll know the answer. Moreover, you will know what you want it to be.

Except for the Introduction and the first and last chapters, you can read this book in any order you wish. The topics are the very issues Doctors face daily in their practice. You know what they are: People, Money, Management, and many more.

Good reading.

Michael E. Gerber
Petaluma, California
January 2003

INTRODUCTION

July 2001. A front-page headline in a Sonoma
County, California, newspaper caught my eye: "Ten
Percent Fewer Doctors in County Since 1995."

The lead offered an explanation: "The number of
Doctors . . . has dropped to levels not seen in two decades, with frustrations over managed care and low
insurance reimbursements cited as major reasons for
discontent, according to a survey of doctors."

How is this possible? The article focuses on a
county that is God's own real estate—wine country
with a nearly perfect climate. From just about everybody's perspective, it is an idyllic place to live. Why,
then, are Doctors getting out?

Actually, I'm not at all surprised. I know a Doctor—let's call him Talbot—who would like to get
out. In a revealing moment of desperation, he once
told me, "If my child wanted to become a Doctor, I'd
shoot him." His uncle, also a Doctor, had tried to

warn Talbot, but he didn't listen. Now all Talbot wants to do is work in his vineyard. He's one depressed guy. The only time he gets excited is when he's talking about wine.

But what exactly is Talbot's problem? Money? No. After 30 years of working with small businesses, many of them medical practices, I'm convinced that the medical malaise experienced by Talbot and countless other doctors is not just a money matter. It's much more than that.

As you already know, I'm not a medical professional; I'm a business professional. But I have more in common with medical professionals than I do with business professionals. Everything I've done in my career in business has had more to do with the value of *life* than the value of *business*.

That's my purpose here. To address the value of *your* life, not only the life of a medical professional but the life of you as a human being. It's my contention that the vast majority of medical professionals today are spending this life fruitlessly—less enjoyably than ever in the history of modern medicine, with less appreciation from patients, less appreciation from the public, and less appreciation from their families.

It's no secret that the life of a medical professional today is one of continuous and often bone-crushing frustration. Despite their medical knowledge and continuous improvements in medical science, most

Doctors are ill at ease with the daily job of bringing medicine to their patients and joy to their work.

The reason for this frustration? Unlike what most medical practitioners will tell you, I suggest that it's not managed care. It's not insurance companies. It's not the patients. And it's not the hard work.

The frustration most Doctors are experiencing has nothing to do with the increasing conflict between the *business* of medicine and the *practice* of medicine. Quite the contrary. That's why, I believe, the solutions created to solve the enormous problems of health care today have failed. The problem of contemporary medicine has its roots at the very beginning.

Let's dig deeper. Let's go back to medical school.

Can you remember that far back? You probably had some great teachers who helped you become the fine Doctor you are. But none had the faintest idea what it takes to build a successful medical enterprise. All they understood, and therefore all they ever taught you, was how to be an *effective* rather than a *successful* medical practitioner.

And that's why today we have countless *effective* medical practitioners but very few *successful* ones. Although a *successful* medical practitioner must be effective, an *effective* medical practitioner does not have to be, and in most cases isn't, successful.

An *effective* medical practitioner is capable of performing the medical art with as much certainty and professionalism as possible.

A *successful* medical practitioner works balanced hours, has little stress, leads a rich and rewarding family life, and has an economic life that is diverse, fulfilling, and shows a continuous return on investment.

A *successful* medical practitioner finds time and ways to give back to the community but at little cost to his or her sense of ease. A *successful* medical practitioner is a leader who has more to teach patients than just medicine; a sage; a rich person (in the broadest sense of the word); a strong father, mother, wife, or husband; a friend, teacher, mentor, and spiritually grounded human being; a person who lives beyond the *science* of medicine to fully exemplify the *spirit* of medicine.

That's how Doctors were thought of years ago. Maybe it wasn't even true then, but it's far less true today. And that picture is growing bleaker, not better. Eighty-three percent of Doctors responding to a national survey said practicing medicine is less satisfying now than it was 5 years ago, and 55 percent said they planned to retire early, move away, or leave the profession.

Obviously, something is seriously wrong: The education that medical professionals receive in school doesn't go far enough, deep enough, broad enough. Medical schools don't teach you how to relate to the *enterprise* of medicine or to the *business* of medicine; they only teach you how to relate to the *practice* of medicine. This limited perspective—this failure to understand and appreciate the business and the enterprise of medicine—is the cause of the crisis in medicine.

Let's look at what we mean by *enterprise*.

Those of you who have read my book, *The E-Myth: Why Most Small Businesses Don't Work and What to Do About It,* will recall that every enterprise in the world that really matters is organized into three distinct levels of work: (1) the work of the Entrepreneur, (2) the work of the Manager, and (3) the work of the Technician.

Entrepreneur, Manager, Technician—the relationship between the three is critical as they play themselves out in a true enterprise.

I often say that most *businesses* don't work and most *practices* don't work—the people who own them do. In other words, most medical practices are jobs for the Doctors who own them. Does this sound familiar?

Of course, the Doctor is only one part of the process. In a medical practice, the Doctor is the Technician, the doer, the producer. Not necessarily the *only* Technician but the *Primary* Technician. Without the Doctor, the medical practice couldn't do what it's supposed to do.

In most medical practices, Technicians simply work for a living. They may be paid well for it, but if the practice depends solely on the Technician for its life and vitality, it will suffer for the lack of the other two roles. If the practice is to flourish, the Doctor must also fill the roles of Manager and Entrepreneur. A Technician-dependent practice is an accident waiting to happen. Instead of becoming what it could be—a healthy, vibrant business on its way to becoming a healthy, vibrant enterprise—the Technician-dependent practice is the worst organization in the world. The Doctor, overcome by an entrepreneurial seizure, has started his or her own medical practice, become his or her own boss, and now works for a lunatic!

The result: The Doctor is *doing it, doing it, doing it,* 17 hours a day, 7 days a week, running out of time, patience, and ultimately money. And paying the worst price anyone can pay for the inability to understand what a true practice is, what a true business is, and what a true enterprise is—the price of his or her life.

Understand that this problem is not only true in medicine but in every organization of every size, in every industry in every country in the world. Without the Entrepreneur and the Manager—and the vision, skill, and understanding they bring—a practice, a business, an enterprise is doomed to fail.

And that's why medicine is failing today. It's simply out of balance. Medical practices are primarily created by Technicians suffering from an entrepreneurial seizure; or worse, Managers interested only in the bottom line. Occasionally, they are created by Entrepreneurs who are completely disconnected from the heart of medicine and driven only by the financial opportunities. In any case, these people are killing medicine. And it's dying right before our eyes.

Unless the medical professional community learns how to correct this disaster, it *will* be destroyed, and Doctors will have been as responsible for the demise of medicine as the Managers who don't get it and the Entrepreneurs who never will.

Someone once said, "Be careful what you wish for because you just might get it." Most Doctors I've met can appreciate this thought. Because at some point in their career, they have asked themselves, *Why in the world did I become a Doctor?*

Although I don't know how you've answered that question in the past, I am confident that once you understand the Strategic Thinking laid out in this book, you will answer it differently in the future.

So, let's think it through together. Let's think about those things—Work, People, Money, Time—that make up the world of Doctors everywhere.

Let's think about improving life—or maybe even getting a life—through the development of an extraordinary practice. About getting a life that's *yours.*

CHAPTER ONE

The Story of Keith and Susan

Mind and heart are only different aspects of us.

THE DANCING WU LI MASTERS
GARY ZUKAV

Despite what most Doctors think, every business is a family business. To ignore this truth is to court disaster.

This is true whether or not family members actually work in the business. Whatever their relationship with the business, every member of a Doctor's family will be greatly affected by the decisions a Doctor makes about the business.

Unfortunately, Doctors tend to compartmentalize their lives unless some family members are actively involved in their practice. Doctors see their practice as *separate* from their family. They see their practice as a profession—what they do—and therefore none of their family's business.

"This doesn't concern you," says the Doctor to the spouse.

"I leave business at the office and my family at home," says the Doctor, with blind conviction.

And with equal conviction, I say, "Not true!"

In actuality, your family and practice are inextricably linked to one another. What's happening in your medical practice is also happening at home. Consider the following and ask yourself if each is true:

- If you're angry at work, you're also angry at home.

- If you're out of control in your medical practice, you're equally out of control at home.

- If you're having trouble with money in your medical practice, you're also having trouble with money at home.

- If you have communication problems in your practice, you're also having communication problems at home.

- If you don't trust in your practice, you don't trust at home.

- If you're secretive in your practice, you're equally secretive at home.

And you're paying a huge price for it!

The truth is that your practice and your family are one—and you're the link. Or you should be. Because if you try to keep your practice and your family apart, if you try to keep your practice and your family strangers, you will effectively create two worlds that can never wholeheartedly serve each other. Two worlds that split each other apart.

Let me tell you the story of Keith and Susan.

Keith Roberts and Susan Boga met in college. Participants in an anti-Vietnam sit-in in the chancellor's office, they sat next to each other and talked for hours. Though not a leader of the movement, Keith was one of its fiery orators. Susan thought he was the most dynamic man she had ever met, and soon they were living together.

Though Keith's father, now deceased, had been a doctor, Keith rejected everything his father stood for: rigid discipline, small-town thinking, and medicine. Instead, after graduation he became a landscaper. He loved getting his hands dirty and being his own boss. Still, Susan sensed that something was missing in Keith's life.

Every Christmas, Keith and Susan flew to Iowa to visit Keith's mother. Keith could hardly walk outside without someone approaching him with essentially the same message: "Your father was such a good man. He helped so many people. You must be so proud."

Keith and his father had never been close, so

pride was not the first emotion that came to mind. Anger? His father rarely spoke to him except to criticize. Resentment? His father was rarely at home.

At his mother's house, Keith was drawn to a photo on the mantle. It was a picture of his father, black bag in one hand, bending over to kiss a little boy who was wearing a leg brace. Though that picture had been there for years, he had never really looked at it. Now he stared at it as though for the first time.

Two nights later, Keith announced that he wanted to go to medical school. Convinced that her husband was meant for great things, Susan readily agreed, promising her support. Through four years of medical school and two years of residency, she worked various jobs to keep them afloat.

Right out of school, Keith—Dr. Roberts—went to work for a medium-size medical practice near Sacramento, California. Soon afterward, Keith and Susan had a daughter. Those were good years. They dearly loved each other, were active members of their church, participated in community organizations, and spent quality time together. All in all, they considered themselves one of the most fortunate families they knew.

But work became troublesome. Dr. Roberts grew increasingly frustrated with the way the practice was run. "I want to go into business for myself," he announced one night. "I want to start my own practice."

Keith and Susan spent many nights talking about the move. Was it something they could afford? Did Keith really have the skills necessary to make a medical practice a success? Were there enough patients to go around? What impact would such a move have on their lifestyle, on their daughter, on their relationship? They asked all the questions they needed to answer before going into business for themselves.

Finally, tired of talking and confident that he could handle whatever he might face, Keith committed to starting his own practice. Because she loved Keith and did not want to stand in his way, Susan went along, offering her own commitment to help.

Thus began the practice of Dr. Roberts. He quit his job, took out a second mortgage on their home, and leased a small office.

In the beginning, it went well. A building boom had hit the town, and new families were pouring into the area. Dr. Roberts had no trouble getting new patients. His practice expanded, quickly outgrowing his waiting room.

Within a year, the practice employed an office manager, a receptionist, and a bookkeeper to take care of the money. Keith was ecstatic with the progress his young practice had made. He celebrated by buying a new Mercedes and joining a country club.

Of course, managing a practice was more complicated and time-consuming than working for someone else. Dr. Roberts not only supervised all the jobs his people did but was forever looking for work to keep them busy. In his spare time, he spoke with insurance companies, went to the bank, and waded through piles of paperwork. Dr. Roberts also found himself spending more and more time on the telephone, mostly dealing with patient complaints and nurturing relationships.

As the months went by and more and more patients came through the door, Dr. Roberts had to spend even more time just trying to keep his head above water.

By the end of its second year, the practice, now employing four full-time and two part-time people, had moved to a larger office downtown. The demands on Dr. Roberts's time had grown with the practice.

The Doctor began leaving home earlier in the morning, returning home later at night. He drank more. He rarely saw his daughter anymore. For the most part, he was resigned to the problem. He saw the hard work as essential to building the "sweat equity" he had long heard about.

Money was also becoming a problem for Dr. Roberts. Although the practice was growing like crazy, money always seemed scarce when it was really needed. He had discovered that insurance companies were often slow to pay.

When Dr. Roberts had worked for someone else, he had been paid twice a month; in his own practice, he often had to wait, sometimes for months. He was still owed money on billings he had submitted more than 90 days before.

When he complained to late-paying insurers, it fell on deaf ears. They would shrug, smile, and promise to do their best, adding, "But you know how business is."

Of course, no matter how slowly Dr. Roberts got paid, he still had to pay *his* people. This became a relentless problem. Keith often felt like a juggler dancing on a tightrope. A fire burned in his stomach day and night.

Making it worse, Keith began to feel that Susan was insensitive to his troubles. Not that he often talked to his wife about the practice. "Business is business" was Keith's mantra. "It's my responsibility to handle things and Susan's responsibility to take care of our daughter, the house, and me."

Susan's seeming lack of understanding rankled Keith. Didn't she see that he had a practice to take care of? That he was doing it all for his family? Apparently not.

As time went on, Dr. Roberts became more consumed and frustrated by his practice. When he went off on his own, he remembered saying, "I don't like people telling me what to do." But people were still telling him what to do. Just yesterday, his office had to get an insurance authorization for a $6 blood test. It required a long-distance call and several minutes on hold.

Not surprisingly, Susan grew more frustrated by her husband's lack of communication, his seeming lack of interest in her and their daughter. She persisted in quizzing him about what was going on at work, why he always looked so stressed. She pressed him to spend more time with his family.

The bookkeeper, Devin, was also becoming a problem. Devin never seemed to have the financial information Dr. Roberts needed to make decisions about payroll and general operating expenses, let alone how much money was available for Keith and Susan's living expenses.

When questioned, Devin would shift his gaze to his feet and say, "Listen, Doctor, I've got a lot more to do around here than you can imagine. It'll take a little more time. Just don't press me, okay?"

Overwhelmed by his own work, Dr. Roberts usually backed off. The last thing he wanted was to upset Devin and have to do the books himself. He could also empathize with what Devin was going through, given their growth over the past year.

Late at night in his office, Dr. Roberts would sometimes recall his first years out of medical school. He missed the simple life. Then, as quickly as the thoughts came, they would vanish. He had work to do and no time for daydreaming. "Having my own medical practice is a great thing," he would remind himself. "I simply have to apply myself, as I did in school, and get on with the job. I have to work as hard as I always have when something needed to get done."

Dr. Roberts began to live most of his life inside his head. He began to distrust his people. They never seemed to work hard enough or to care about his practice as much as he did. If he wanted to get something done, he usually had to do it himself.

Then one day, the office manager, Karen, quit in a huff, frustrated by the amount of work he was demanding of her. Dr. Roberts was left with a desk full of papers, a waiting room full of patients, and a telephone that wouldn't stop ringing.

Clueless about the work Karen had done, Dr. Roberts was overwhelmed by having to pick up the pieces of a job he didn't understand. His world turned upside down. He felt like a stranger in his own practice.

Why had he been such a fool? Why hadn't he taken the time to learn what Karen did in the office? Why had he waited until now? Ever the trooper, Dr. Roberts plowed into Karen's job with everything he could muster. What he found shocked him. Karen's work space was a disaster area! Her desk drawers were a jumble of papers, pens, pencils, erasers, rubber bands, envelopes, business cards, and candy.

"What was she thinking?" the Doctor raged.

When he got home that night, even later than usual, he got into a shouting match with Susan. He settled it by storming out of the house to get a drink.

Didn't anybody understand him? Didn't anybody care what he was going through?

He returned home only when he was sure Susan was asleep. He slept on the couch. He left early in the morning before anyone was awake. He was in no mood for questions or arguments.

When Dr. Roberts got to the office, he immediately headed for the medicine cabinet. . . .

What lessons can we draw from Keith and Susan's story? As I've already emphatically said, every business is a family business. Every business profoundly touches every family member, even those not working in the business. Every business either gives to the family or takes from the family, just as individual family members do.

If the business takes, the family is always the first to pay the price.

In order for Dr. Roberts to free himself from his prison, he first had to admit his vulnerability. He had to confess to himself and his family that he really didn't know enough about his own practice and how to grow it.

Dr. Roberts had tried to do it all himself. Had he succeeded, had the practice supported his family in the style he imagined, he would have burst with pride. Instead, he had unwittingly isolated himself, thereby achieving the exact opposite of what he sought.

He destroyed his life—and his family's life along with it.

Repeat after me: "Every business is a family business."

Are you like Dr. Roberts? I believe that all Doctors share a common soul with him. You must learn that a business is only a business. It is not your life. But it is also true that your business can have a profoundly negative impact on your life unless you learn how to do it differently than most Doctors do it. Differently than Dr. Roberts did it.

Dr. Roberts's practice could have served his and his family's life. But for that to happen, the Doctor would have had to learn how to master his practice.

Instead, Dr. Roberts's practice consumed him. Lacking a true understanding of the essential strategic thinking that would have allowed him to create something unique, Dr. Roberts and his family were doomed before he even opened his doors.

This book contains the secrets that Dr. Roberts should have known.

Let's start with the subject of *money.*

CHAPTER TWO

On the Subject of Money

If a rich man is proud of his wealth, he should not
be praised until it is known how he employs it.

SOCRATES

Had Keith and Susan first considered the subject of
money as we will here, their lives would have been
radically different.

Money is on the tip of every Doctor's tongue, on
the edge (or at the center) of every Doctor's thoughts,
intruding on every part of a Doctor's life.

With money consuming so much energy, why do
so few Doctors handle it well? Why was Dr. Roberts,
like so many Doctors, willing to entrust his financial
affairs to a relative stranger? Why is money scarce for
most Doctors? Why is there less money than
expected? And yet the demand for money is *always*
greater than anticipated.

What is it about money that is so elusive, so complicated, so compelling yet so difficult to control? Why is it that every Doctor I've ever met *hates* to deal with the subject of money? Why are Doctors always tardy in facing money problems? And why are they constantly obsessed with the need for more of it?

Some of the reasons are obvious. Doctors spend most of their lives studying medicine, then practicing it without a chance to study the economics of medicine. And after an all-nighter in the operating room followed by an office full of patients, it's not hard to understand why Doctors pay little attention to the dynamics of money.

I'm reminded of a Henny Youngman line that resonates with truth: "I've got all the money I'll ever need—if I die by four o'clock this afternoon."

Money—you can't live with it and you can't live without it. But you better understand it and get your people to understand it. Because until you do, money problems will eat your practice for lunch!

You don't need an accountant or financial planner to do this. You simply need to prod your people to relate to money very personally. From Doctor to receptionist, they should all understand the financial impact of what they do every day in relationship to the profit and loss of the organization.

And so you must teach your people to think like owners, not like nurses or file clerks or receptionists. You must teach them to operate like personal profit centers, with a sense of how their work fits in with the practice as a whole.

You must involve everyone in the practice with the topic of money—how it works, where it goes, how much is left, and how much everybody gets at the end of the day. You also must teach them about the four kinds of money created by the practice.

THE FOUR FACTORS OF MONEY

In the context of owning, operating, developing, and exiting from a medical practice, four highly integrated factors govern the subject of money: Income, Profit, Flow, and Equity.

Failure to distinguish how the four factors of money play themselves out in your practice is a surefire recipe for disaster.

Important Note: Do not talk to your accountants, bookkeepers, or office managers about what follows; it will only confuse them and you. This information comes from the real-life experiences of tens of thousands of small business owners, including Doctors, most of whom were hopelessly confused about money when I met them. Once they understood and accepted the following principles, they developed a clarity about money that could only be called enlightened.

The First Factor of Money: Income

Income is the money Doctors are paid by their business for doing a job *in* the business. It's what they get paid for going to work every day.

Clearly, if Doctors didn't do their job, others would have to, and *they* would be paid the money the business currently pays the Doctor. Income, then, has nothing to do with *ownership;* it has to do with *employee-ship.*

To the Doctor-as-*Employee,* Income is naturally the most important form money can take. To the Doctor-as-*Owner,* Income is the *least* important form money can take.

Most important; least important. Do you see the conflict? The conflict between the Doctor-as-Employee and the Doctor-as-Owner?

We'll deal with this conflict later. For now, just know that it is potentially the most paralyzing conflict in a Doctor's life.

Resolving this conflict, as we intend to do in this book, will set you free!

The Second Factor of Money: Profit

Profit is what's left over after a practice has done its job effectively and efficiently. If there is no Profit, the practice is doing something wrong.

However, just because the practice shows a Profit does not mean it is necessarily doing all the right things in the right way. Instead, it just means that *something* was done right during or preceding the period in which the Profit was earned.

The important issue here is whether the Profit was intentional or accidental. If it happened by accident (which most Profit does), don't take credit for it. You'll live to regret your impertinence.

If Profit happened intentionally, take all the credit you want. You've earned it. Because profit created intentionally, rather than by accident, is replicable—again and again. And your practice's ability to repeat its performance is the most critical ability it can have.

As you'll soon see, the value of money is a function of your practice's ability to produce it in predictable amounts at an above-average return on investment.

Profit can be understood only in the context of your practice's purpose, as opposed to *your* purpose. Profit, then, fuels the forward motion of the practice that produces it. This is accomplished in four ways:

1. Profit is *investment capital* that feeds and supports growth.

2. Profit is *bonus capital* that rewards people for exceptional work.

3. Profit is *operating capital* that shores up money shortfalls.

4. Profit is *return-on-investment capital* that rewards you, the Doctor-owner, for taking risks.

Without Profit, a practice cannot subsist, much less grow. Profit is the fuel of progress.

If a practice misuses or abuses Profit, however, the penalty is much like having no Profit at all. Imagine the plight of a Doctor who has way too much return-on-investment capital and not enough investment capital, bonus capital, and operating capital.

Are you aware of this imbalance in your practice?

The Third Factor of Money: Flow

Flow is what money *does* in a practice rather than what money *is*. Whether the practice is large or small, money tends to move erratically through it, like a pinball. One minute it's there; the next minute it's not.

Flow can be even more critical to a practice's survival than Profit, because a practice can produce a Profit and still be short of money. Has this ever happened to you? It's called Profit on Paper rather than in fact.

No matter how large your practice, if the money isn't there when it's needed, you're threatened, regardless of how much Profit you've made. Of course, you can borrow it. But as you know, money acquired in dire circumstances is almost always the most expensive kind of money you can get.

Knowing where money is and where it will be when you need it is a critically important task of both the Doctor-as-Employee and the Doctor-as-Owner.

RULES OF FLOW

You will learn no more important lesson than the huge impact Flow can have on the health and survival of your practice, let alone your business or enterprise. The following rules will help you understand why this subject is so critical.

The First Rule of Flow states that your Income Statement is static, while the Flow is dynamic. Your Income Statement is a snapshot, while the Flow is a moving picture. So, while your Income Statement is an excellent tool for analyzing your practice *after* the fact, it's a poor tool for managing it in the heat of the moment.

Your Income Statement tells you (1) how much money you're spending and where, and (2) how much money you're receiving and from where.

Flow gives you the same information as the Income Statement, plus it tells you *when* you're spending and receiving money—that is, Flow is an Income Statement moving through time. And that is the key to understanding Flow. It is about management in real time. How much is coming in? How much is going out? You'd like to know this daily, or even by the hour if possible. Never by the week or month.

You must be able to forecast Flow. You must have a Flow Plan that helps you gain a clear vision of the money that's out there next month and the month after that.

You must also pinpoint what your needs will be in the future. Ultimately, however, when it comes to Flow, the action is always in the moment.

It's about now!

Managing Flow takes attention to detail. But when Flow is managed, your life takes on an incredible sheen. You're in charge! You're swimming with the current, not against it.

Unfortunately, few Doctors pay any attention to Flow until it stops and slow pay becomes no-pay. They are oblivious to this kind of detail until, say, insurance companies announce that they won't pay for this or that. That gets their attention because the expenses keep on coming.

When it comes to money, to Flow, most Doctors are flying by the proverbial seat of their pants. No matter how many people you hire to take care of your money, until you change the way you think about it, you will always be out of luck. No one can do this for you.

The Second Rule of Flow states that money seldom moves as you expect it to. But you do have the power to change that provided you understand the two primary sources of money as it comes in and goes out of your practice.

The more control you have over the *sources* of money, the more control you have over its Flow. These sources are both inside and outside of your practice.

Money comes from *outside* your practice in the form of receivables, reimbursements, investments, and loans.

Money comes from *inside* your practice in the form of payables, taxes, capital investments, and payroll. These are the costs associated with attracting patients, delivering your services, operations, and so forth.

Few Doctors see the money going *out* of their practice as a source of money, but it is.

When considering how to spend money in your practice, you can save—and therefore make—money in three ways:

1. Do it more effectively.

2. Do it more efficiently.

3. Stop doing it altogether.

By identifying the money sources inside and outside of your practice, and then applying these methods, you will be immeasurably better at controlling the Flow in your practice.

But what are these sources? They include how you:

- Manage your services

- Buy supplies and equipment

- Compensate your people

- Plan people's use of time

- Determine the direct cost of your services

- Increase the time you spend seeing patients

- Manage your work

- Collect reimbursements and receivables

And countless more. In fact, every task performed in your practice (and ones you haven't yet learned how to perform) can be done more efficiently and effectively, dramatically reducing the cost of doing business. In the process, you will create more Income, produce more Profit, and balance the Flow.

Oh, what a happy day that will be.

The Fourth Factor of Money: Equity

Sadly, few Doctors fully appreciate the value of Equity in their practice. Yet, Equity is the second most valuable asset any Doctor will ever possess. (The *first* most valuable—your life—is discussed in Chapters One and Eleven.)

> **EQUITY** is the financial value placed on your practice by a prospective buyer of your practice.

Thus, your *practice* is your most important product, not your services. Because your practice has the power to set you free. That's right. Once you sell your practice—providing you get what you want for it—you're free!

Of course, to enhance your Equity, to increase your practice's value, you have to build it right. You have to build a practice that works. A practice that can become a true business and a business that can become a true enterprise. A practice/business/enterprise that can produce Income, Profit, Flow, and Equity better than any other practice/business/enterprise can.

To accomplish that, your practice must be designed so that it can do what it does systematically, predictably, every single time.

The Story of McDonald's

Let me tell you the most unlikely story anyone has ever told you about the successful building of a medical practice, business, and enterprise. Let me tell you the story of Ray Kroc.

Bear with me now. I know what you're thinking: What is Michael Gerber talking about? How can he compare a medical practice to a hamburger stand? I'm not in the hamburger business; I'm a medical professional.

Yes, you are. But by practicing medicine as you have been taught, you have abandoned any chance to expand your reach, to touch more patients, to improve medical services the way they must be improved if medicine—and your life—is going to be transformed.

In Ray Kroc's story lies the answer. Please follow closely. Because, Doctor, your life depends on it.

Ray Kroc called his first McDonald's restaurant "a little money machine." That's why thousands of franchisees bought it. And the reason it worked? Ray Kroc demanded consistency. So that a hamburger in Philadelphia would be an advertisement for one in Peoria. In fact, no matter where you bought an early McDonald's hamburger, the meat patty was guaranteed to weigh exactly 1.6 ounces, with a diameter of 3⅝ inches. It was in the McDonald's handbook.

Did Ray Kroc succeed? You know he did! And so can you, once you understand his methods. Consider just one part of Ray Kroc's story.

In 1954, Ray Kroc made his living selling the five-spindle Multimixer milkshake machine. He heard about a hamburger stand in San Bernardino, California, which had eight of his machines in operation, meaning it could make 40 shakes simultaneously. That he had to see.

Kroc flew from Chicago to Los Angeles, then drove 60 miles to San Bernardino. As he sat in his car outside Mac and Dick McDonald's restaurant, he watched as lunch customers lined up for bags of hamburgers.

In a revealing moment, Kroc approached a strawberry blonde in a yellow convertible. As he later described it, "It was not her sex appeal but the obvious relish with which she devoured the hamburger that made my pulse begin to hammer with excitement."

Passion.

Actually, it was the french fry that truly captured his heart. Before the 1950s, it was almost impossible to buy fries of consistent quality. Ray Kroc changed all that. "The french fry," he once wrote, "would become almost sacrosanct for me, its preparation a ritual to be followed religiously."

Passion and preparation.

The potatoes had to be just so—top-quality Idaho russets, 8 ounces apiece, deep-fried to a golden brown, and salted with a shaker that, as Kroc put it, kept going "like a Salvation Army girl's tambourine."

As Kroc soon learned, potatoes too high in water content—and even top-quality Idaho russets varied greatly in water content—will come out soggy when fried. And so Kroc sent out teams of workers, armed with hydrometers, to make sure all his suppliers were producing potatoes in the optimal solids range of 20 to 23 percent.

Preparation and passion. Passion and preparation. Look up these words in the dictionary, and you'll see Ray Kroc's picture. Can you see your picture there?

Do you understand what Ray Kroc did? Do you see why he was able to sell thousands of franchises? Kroc knew the true value of Equity, and, unlike Keith, Kroc went to work *on* his business rather than *in* his business. He knew the hamburger wasn't his product—McDonald's was!

He created a foolproof, predictable practice that would work once it was sold, no matter who bought it. A systems-dependent practice, not a people-dependent practice. Most business founders believe the success of a business resides in the success of the product it sells. Kroc knew the real value lies in the brand name—Cadillac, Coca-Cola, McDonald's.

So what does *your* Doctor's practice need to do to become a little money machine? What is the passion that will drive you to build a practice that works—a turnkey system like Ray Kroc's?

The McDonald's franchise is a metaphor for a way of rethinking medicine, for the practice, business, and enterprise of medicine. In other words, a seamless system that reflects the passion the Doctor has for providing care without succumbing to the dehumanization of the present situation. Ironically, the McDonald's system is the only way to inject humanity into medicine.

Equity and the Turnkey System

What's a turnkey system? And why is it so valuable to you? To better understand it, let's look at another example of a turnkey system that worked to perfection: the recordings of Frank Sinatra.

Note that I am again asking you to take a leap of faith. I'm asking you to become a generalist rather than a specialist; to think metaphorically rather than literally; to think like an entrepreneur rather than a technician. In this way, you will transcend the work of medicine and learn how to make medicine work like it's never worked before.

Frank Sinatra's records were to him as McDonald's restaurants were to Ray Kroc. As your practice can be to you. Those records were part of a turnkey system that allowed Sinatra to sing to hundreds of millions of people without ever having to be there himself.

Sinatra's recordings were a dependable turnkey system that worked predictably, systematically, and effortlessly to produce the same results every single time—no matter where they were played, no matter who was listening.

Regardless of where Frank Sinatra was, his records just kept on producing Income, Profit, Flow, and Equity, over and over . . . and still do! Sinatra needed only to produce the prototype recording and the system did the rest.

Kroc's McDonald's is another prototypical turnkey solution, addressing everything McDonald's needs to do in a basic, systematic way so that anyone properly trained by McDonald's can successfully reproduce the same results.

And this is where you'll realize your Equity Opportunity: in the way your practice does business; in the way your practice systematically does what you intend it to do; in the development of your turnkey system—a system that works even in the hands of ordinary people (and Doctors less experienced than you) to produce extraordinary results.

Remember:

- If you want to build vast Equity in your practice, then go to work *on* your practice, building it into a business that works every single time.

- Go to work *on* your practice to build a totally integrated turnkey system that delivers exactly what you promised every single time.

- Go to work *on* your practice to package it and make it stand out from the Doctors' practices you see everywhere else.

Here is the most important idea you will ever hear about your practice and what it can potentially provide for you:

The value of your equity is directly proportional to how well your practice works. And how well your practice works is directly proportional to the effectiveness of the systems

you have put into place, upon which the operation of your practice depends.

Money, Happiness, Life—they all come down to how well your practice works. Not how well you work. Whether money takes the form of Income, Profit, Flow, or Equity, the amount of it—and how much of it stays with you—will always depend on how well your practice works. Not on your people, not on you, but on the system.

Your practice holds the secret to more money. Are you ready to learn how to find it?

Earlier in this chapter, I alerted you to the inevitable conflict between the Doctor-as-Employee and the Doctor-as-Owner. It's a battle between the part of you working *in* the practice and the part of you working *on* the practice. Between the part of you working for Income and the part of you working for Equity.

Here's how to resolve this conflict:

1. Be honest with yourself about whether you're filling *employee* shoes or *owner* shoes.

2. As your practice's key employee, determine the most effective way to do the job you're doing, *and then document that job.*

3. Once you've documented the job, create a strategy for replacing yourself with someone else (another Doctor, or, even better, a paraprofessional) who will then use your documented system exactly as you do.

4. Use your new employees to manage the newly delegated system. Improve the system by quantifying its effectiveness over time.

5. Repeat this process throughout your practice wherever you are acting as employee rather than owner. Leave behind dedicated people using your effective systems.

6. Learn to distinguish between ownership work and employee-ship work every step of the way.

Master these methods, come face to face with the significant difference between the Four Factors of Money, develop an interest in how money works in your practice, and then watch the money flow in!

Now let's take another step in our Strategic Thinking Process. Let's look at the subject of *planning.*

CHAPTER THREE

On the Subject of Planning

> People in an organization operating from a
> creative mode . . . approach planning first by
> determining what they truly want to create,
> thus in essence becoming true to themselves.
>
> *THE PATH OF LEAST RESISTANCE*
> ROBERT FRITZ

Another obvious oversight revealed in Keith and Susan's story was the absence of true planning.

Every Doctor starting his or her business must have a plan. You shouldn't even begin to see a patient without one. But, of course, every Doctor does. In this chapter, we discuss how to plan more effectively.

A Doctor lacking a business vision is simply someone who goes to work every day. Someone who is just doing it, doing it, doing it. Busy, busy, busy. Maybe making money, maybe not. Maybe getting something out of life, maybe not. Taking chances without really taking control.

The plan tells anyone who needs to know *how we do things here*. The plan defines the Objective and the process by which you will attain it. The plan encourages you to organize tasks into functions, and then helps people grasp the logic of each of those functions. This in turn permits you to bring new employees up to speed quickly.

There are numerous books and seminars on the subject of Practice Management, but they focus on making you a better Doctor. I want to teach you something else that you've never been taught before: how to be a manager and an entrepreneur. It has nothing to do with conventional practice management and everything to do with thinking like an entrepreneur.

THE PLANNING TRIANGLE

As we discussed in the Foreword, every medical practice is a company, every medical business is a company, and every medical enterprise is a company. Yet the difference between the three is extraordinary. Although the *business* of all three may be health care, how they do what they do is completely different.

The trouble with most health care companies owned by Doctors is that they are dependent on the Doctor. That's because they're a practice—the smallest, most limited form a company can take. Practices are formed around the technician, whether Doctor or roofer.

You may choose in the beginning to form a practice, but you should understand its limitations. The company called a *practice* depends on the owner—that is, the Doctor. The company called a *business* depends on other people plus a system by which that business does what it does. Once your practice becomes a business, you can replicate it, turning it into an *enterprise.*

Consider the offices of Joanne Jones Surgical Operations. The patients don't come in asking for Dr. Jones; they ask for Surgery. Although Dr. Jones is the best hemorrhoid surgeon around, she can only handle so many cases a day; yet she wants to offer her high-quality services to more people in the community. If she has reliable systems in place—systems that any qualified technician can learn to use—she has created a business and it can be replicated. Dr. Jones can then go on to offer her services—which demand her guidance, not her presence—in dozens of medical settings. She can open dozens of medical companies, none of which need Dr. Jones, except in the role of entrepreneur.

Is your medical company going to be a practice, a business, or an enterprise? Planning is crucial to answering this all-important question. Whatever you choose to do must be communicated by your plan, which is really three interrelated plans in one. We call it the Planning Triangle, and it consists of:

The Business Plan

The Practice Plan

The Completion Plan

The three plans form a triangle, with the Business Plan at the base, the Practice Plan in the center, and the Completion Plan at the apex.

THE PLANNING TRIANGLE

The Business Plan determines *who* you are (the business), the Practice Plan determines *what* you do (the specific focus of your practice), and the Completion Plan determines *how* you do it (the fulfillment process).

By looking at the Planning Triangle, we see that the three critical plans are interconnected. The connection between them is established by asking the following questions:

1. **Who are we?**

2. **What do we do?**

3. **How do we do it?**

Who are we? is purely a Strategic Question.

What do we do? is both a Strategic and a Tactical Question.

How do we do it? is both a Strategic and a Tactical Question.

Strategic Questions shape the vision and destiny of your business, of which your practice is only one essential component. Tactical Questions turn that vision into reality.

Let me restate that your business and your practice are not the same thing. Your practice is only one part of your business.

Strategic Questions provide the foundation for Tactical Questions, just as the base provides the foundation for the middle and apex of your Planning Triangle.

First ask: What do we do and how do we do it . . . *strategically?*

And then: What do we do and how do we do it . . . *tactically?*

Let's look at how the three plans will help you develop your practice.

The Business Plan

Your Business Plan will determine what you choose to do in your practice and the way you choose to do it. Without a Business Plan, your practice can do little more than survive. And even that will take luck.

Without a Business Plan you're treading water in a deep pool with no shore in sight. You're working against the natural flow.

I'm not talking about the traditional Business Plan that is taught in business schools. No. This Business Plan reads like a story, the most important story you will ever tell.

Your Business Plan must clearly describe:

- The business you are creating

- The purpose it will serve

- The vision it will pursue

- The process through which you will turn that vision into a reality

- The way money will be used to realize your vision

Build your Business Plan with *business* language,

not *practice* language (the language of the Doctor, nurse, radiologist, whomever). Make sure the plan focuses on matters of interest to your lenders and shareholders rather than just your technicians. It should detail both the market and the strategy through which you intend to become a leader in that market, not as a Doctor but as a business enterprise. It should rely on demographics and psychographics to tell you who buys and why. It should include projections for Return on Investment and Return on Equity.

The Business Plan, though absolutely essential, is only one of three critical plans every Doctor needs to create and then implement to avoid going on life support.

The Practice Plan

The Practice Plan includes everything a Doctor needs to know, have, and do in order to deliver his or her promise to a patient on time, every time.

Every task should prompt you to ask three questions:

1. What do I need to know?

2. What do I need to have?

3. What do I need to do?

■ *What do I need to know?* What information do I need to satisfy my promise on time, every time, exactly as promised? In order to recognize what you need to know, you must understand the expectations and limitations of others, including patients, administrators, nurses, and employees. Are you clear on those expectations? Don't make the mistake of assuming you know. Instead, create a Need-to-Know Checklist to make sure you ask all the necessary questions.

Need-to-Know Checklist

■ What are the expectations of my patients?

■ What are the expectations of my administrators?

■ What are the expectations of my nurses and technicians?

■ What are the expectations of my staff?

■ *What do I need to have?* This question raises the issue of resources—namely Money, Equipment, People, and Time. If you don't have the right equipment, how can you fill the patient's expectations as promised? If you don't have enough money to finance operations, how can you fulfill those expectations without creating cash-flow problems? If you don't have enough trained people, what happens then? And if you don't have the time to manage your practice, what happens when you can't be in two places at once?

Don't assume that you can get what you need when you need it; most often, you can't. And even if you can get it at the last minute, you will pay dearly for it.

■ *What do I need to do?* The focus here is on actions to be started and finished. What do I need to do to fulfill the expectations of this patient on time, every time, exactly as promised? For example, what exactly are the steps to perform when seeing a patient with, say, an upper respiratory problem or when scheduling a hernia repair? Your patients fall into discreet categories, and those categories make up your practice. The best practices will invariably focus on fewer and fewer categories as they discover the importance of doing one thing better than anyone else.

Answering the question *What do I need to do?* demands a series of Action Plans, including:

■ The objective to be achieved

■ The standards by which you will know that the objective has been achieved

■ The Benchmarks you need to reach in order for the objective to be achieved

■ The function/person accountable for the completion of the Benchmarks

- The budget for the completion of each Benchmark

- The time in which each Benchmark must be completed

Your Action Plans should become the foundation for the Completion Plans you must create in order to assure that everything you do is not only realistic but can be managed.

The Completion Plan

If the Practice Plan gives you results and provides you with standards, the Completion Plan tells you everything you need to know about every Benchmark in the Practice Plan—that is, how you're going to fulfill patient expectations on time, every time, as promised. How you're going to arrange a phlebotomy, issue a prescription, or educate a patient about her diabetes.

The Completion Plan is essentially the operations manual, providing information about the details of doing Tactical Work. It is a guide to tell the people responsible for doing that work exactly how to do it.

Every Completion Plan becomes a part of the knowledge base of your business. No Completion Plan goes to waste. Every Completion Plan becomes an open book, a textbook, to explain to new staff or new physicians joining your team how your practice operates in a way that distinguishes it from all other Doctors' practices.

Take McDonald's, for example (I know this seems a stretch, but bear with me). The Completion Plan for making a Big Mac is explicitly described in the *McDonald's Operations Manual,* as is every Completion Plan needed to run a McDonald's business.

The Completion Plan for a Doctor might include the step-by-step details of how to perform a colonoscopy—in contrast to how everyone else has learned to do it. Of course, every medical practice has learned how to use a scale. They've learned to do it the same way everyone else has learned to do it. But if you are going to stand out as unique in the minds of your patients, employees, and others, you must invent your own way of doing even ordinary things. You must constantly raise the questions *How do we do it here? How should we do it here?*

The quality of your answers will determine how effectively you distinguish your business from every other Doctor's business.

Benchmarks

You can measure the movement of your practice—from what it is today to what it will be in the future—using Business Benchmarks. These are the goals you want your business to achieve during its lifetime.

Your many Benchmarks should include the following:

- Financial Benchmarks

- Emotional Benchmarks (the impact your practice will have on everyone who comes into contact with it)

- Performance Benchmarks

- Patient Benchmarks (Who are they? Why do they come to you? What will your practice give them that no one else will?)

- Employee Benchmarks (How do you grow people? How do you find people who want to grow? How do you create a school in your practice that will teach your people skills they can't learn anywhere else?)

Your Business Benchmarks will reflect (1) the position your practice will hold in the minds and hearts of your patients, employees, investors, and suppliers, and (2) how you intend to make that position a reality through the systems you develop.

Your Benchmarks will describe how your management team will take shape and what systems you will need to develop so that your managers, just like McDonald's managers, will be able to produce the results for which they will be held accountable.

BENEFITS OF THE PLANNING TRIANGLE

By implementing the Planning Triangle, you will discover:

- What your practice will look, act, and feel like when it's fully evolved

- When that's going to happen

- How much money you will make

And much more.

These, then, are the primary purposes of the Three Critical Plans: (1) to clarify precisely what needs to be done to get what the Doctor wants from practice and life, and (2) to define the specific steps by which it will happen.

First *this* must happen, then *that* must happen. One, two, three. By monitoring your progress, step by step, you can determine whether you're on the right track.

That's what planning is all about. It's about creating a standard—a yardstick—against which you can measure your performance.

Failing to create such a standard is like throwing a straw into a hurricane. Who knows where it will land?

Have you taken the leap? Have you accepted that the

word *business* and the word *practice* are not synonymous? That a practice relies on the Doctor and a business relies on other people plus a system? Because most Doctors are control freaks, 99 percent of today's medical companies are practices, not businesses. The result, as my friend Dr. Kivett says, is that "Doctors are spending all day stamping out fires when all around them the forest is ablaze. The business is out of touch, and that doctor better take control of the practice before someone else does."

Because Doctors are never taught to think like businesspeople, Medical Person is forever at war with Businessperson. This is especially evident in large organizations, where bureaucrats (Businesspeople) often try to control Doctors (Medical People). They usually end up treating each other as combatants. In fact, the single greatest reason Doctors become entrepreneurs is to divorce such bureaucrats and to begin to reinvent the medical enterprise.

Now let's take the next step in our Strategic Odyssey. Let's take a closer look at the subject of *management*.

(To find out exactly what your three critical plans will look like when they're done, go to E-Myth.com and click on "The E-Myth Doctor.")

CHAPTER FOUR

On the Subject of Management

"Control follows awareness."

IN SEARCH OF THE WARRIOR SPIRIT
RICHARD STROZZI HECKLER

Every Doctor, including Dr. Roberts, eventually faces the issue of management. Yet most face it badly.

Why do so many Doctors suffer from a kind of paralysis when it comes to dealing with management? Why are so few able to get their practice to work the way they want it to and to run it on time? Why are their managers (if they have any) seemingly so inept?

There are two main problems. First, the Doctor usually abdicates accountability for management by hiring an office manager. Thus, the Doctor is working hand and glove with someone who is supposed to do the managing. But the Doctor is unmanageable.

The Doctor doesn't think like a manager because he doesn't think he is a manager. He's a Doctor! He rules the roost. And so he gets the office manager to take care of stuff like scheduling appointments, keeping his calendar, collecting receivables, hiring/firing, and much more.

Second, no matter who does the managing, they usually have a completely dysfunctional idea of what it means to manage. They are trying to manage people contrary to what is needed.

We often hear that a good manager must be a "people person." Someone who loves to nourish, figure out, support, care for, teach, baby, monitor, mentor, direct, track, motivate, and, if all else fails, threaten or beat up her people. Don't believe it. Management has far less to do with people than you've been led to believe.

In fact, despite the claims of every management book written by management gurus (who seldom have managed anything), no one, except a few tyrants, has ever learned how to manage people. And the reason is simple: As you probably already know, people are almost impossible to manage. What's more, they are inconsistent, unpredictable, unchangeable, unrepentant, irrepressible, and generally impossible.

The time has come to grasp what management is really all about. Rather than managing *people,* management is really all about managing a *process,* a step-by-step way of doing things, which, combined with other processes, becomes a system. For example:

- The process for on-time scheduling
- The process for answering the telephone
- The process for greeting a patient
- The process for organizing patient files

Thus, a process is the step-by-step way of doing something over time. Considered as a whole, these processes are a system:

The On-Time Scheduling System

The Telephone Answering System

The Patient Greeting System

The File Organization System

Instead of managing people, then, the truly effective manager has been taught a system for managing a process through which people get things done better than they could without one.

More precisely, managers and their people, *together,* manage the processes—the systems—that comprise your business. Management is less about *who* gets things done in your business than about *how* things get done.

In fact, great managers are not fascinated with people but with how things get done through people. Great managers are masters at figuring out how to get things done effectively and efficiently through people using extraordinary systems.

Great managers constantly ask key questions:

- What is the result we intend to produce?

- Are we producing that result every single time?

- If we are producing that result every single time, how could we produce even better results?

- If we're not producing that result every single time, why not?

- Do we lack a system? If so, what would that system look like if we were to create it?

- If we have a system, why aren't we using it?

And so forth.

In short, great managers use a great Management System. A system that shouts out, "This is *how* we manage here!" Not, "This is *who* manages here!"

A great manager can leave the office fully assured

that it will run at least as well as it does when he or she is in the office.

In a truly effective company, *how* you manage is always more important than *who* manages. Provided a system is in place, *how* you manage is transferable, whereas *who* manages isn't. *How* you manage (a system) can be taught, whereas *who* manages can't be taught.

When a business is dependent on *who* manages— Murray, Mary, or Dr. Moe—that business is in serious jeopardy. Because when Murray, Mary, or Dr. Moe leaves, that business has to start over again. What an enormous waste of resources. What an enormous waste of time.

Even worse, when a business is dependent on *who* manages, you can bet all the managers in that business are doing their own thing. What could be more unproductive than 10 managers each managing in a unique way? How in the world could you possibly manage those managers?

The answer is clear: You can't. Because it takes you right back to trying to manage *people* again.

And, as I hope you now know, that's impossible.

In this chapter, I often refer to managers in the plural. I know that most Doctors have only one manager—the office manager. And so you may be thinking that maybe a Management System isn't so important in a small practice. After all, the office manager does whatever an office manager does (and thank God because you don't want to do it).

But if your practice is ever going to turn into the business it could become, and if that business is ever going to turn into the enterprise it could become, then the questions you ask about how the office manager manages your affairs are critical ones. Because until you come to grips with your dual role as owner and key employee, and the relationship your manager has to those two roles, your practice/business/enterprise will never realize its potential. Thus the need for a Management System.

MANAGEMENT SYSTEM

What, then, is a Management System?

The E-Myth says that a Management System is the method by which every manager innovates, quantifies, orchestrates, and monitors the systems through which your practice produces the results you expect.

According to The E-Myth, a manager's job is simple:

> A manager's job is to invent the systems through which the owner's vision is consistently and faithfully manifested at the operating level of the business.

Which brings us right back to the purpose of your

business, to the need for an entrepreneurial vision.

Are you beginning to see what I'm trying to share with you? That your business is one single thing? And that all the subjects we're discussing here— money, planning, your business's story, management, and so on—are all about doing one thing well: the one thing your practice is intended to do, which is to distinguish your medical business from all others.

It's the manager's role to make certain it all fits. And it's your role as entrepreneur to make sure your manager knows what the business is supposed to look, act, and feel like when it's finally done. As clearly as you know how, you must convey to your manager what you know to be true—your vision, your picture of the business when it's finally done. In this way, your vision becomes your manager's marching orders every day he or she reports to work.

Unless that vision is embraced by your manager, you and your people will suffer from the tyranny of routine. And your business will suffer from it, too.

Now let's move on to *people*. Because, as we know, it's people who are causing all our problems.

CHAPTER FIVE

On the Subject of People

The greater part of human pain is
unnecessary. It is self-created as long
as the unobserved mind runs your life.

PRACTICING THE POWER OF NOW
ECKHART TOLLE

Every Doctor I've ever met has complained about
people.

About employees: "They come in late, they go
home early, they have the focus of an antique camera!"

About insurance companies: "They're living in a
nonparallel universe!"

About patients: "They want me to repair 40 years
of bad habits!"

People, people, people. Every Doctor's nemesis.
And at the heart of it all are the people who work for
you.

"By the time I tell them how to do it, I could have done it twenty times myself!" "How come nobody listens to what I say?" "Why is it nobody ever does what I ask them to do?" Does this sound like you?

So what's the problem with people? To answer that, think back to the last time you walked into a Doctor's office. What did you see in the people's faces?

Most people working in medicine are harried. You can see it in their expressions. They're negative. They're bad-spirited. They're humorless. And with good reason. After all, they're surrounded by people who don't feel well and have to wait to see the Doctor. Patients are looking for nurturing, for empathy, for care. And many are either terrified or depressed. They don't want to be there.

Is it any wonder that medical employees are disgruntled? They're surrounded by unhappy people all day. They're answering the same questions all day. And most of the time, the Doctor has no time for them. He or she is too busy leading a dysfunctional life.

Working with people brings great joy—and monumental frustration. And so it is with Doctors and their people. But why? And what can we do about it?

Let's look at the typical Doctor—who this person is and isn't.

Most Doctors are unprepared to use other people

to get results. Not because they can't find people but because they are fixated on getting the results themselves. In other words, most Doctors are not the businesspeople they *need* to be but *technicians suffering from an entrepreneurial seizure!*

Am I talking about you? What were *you* doing before you became an entrepreneur?

Were you a pediatrician working for an HMO? Or a gynecologist? Or a podiatrist?

Didn't you imagine owning your own practice as the way out?

Didn't you think that because you knew how to do the technical work, because you knew so much about children or women or feet that you were automatically prepared to create a business that does that type of work?

Didn't you figure that by creating your own practice you could dump the boss once and for all? How else to get rid of that impossible person, the one driving you crazy, the one who never let you do your own thing, the one who was the main reason you decided to take the leap into a business of your own?

Didn't you start your own business so that you could become your own boss? And didn't you imagine that once you became your own boss, you would be free to do whatever you wanted to do—and to take home *all* the money?

Honestly, isn't that what you imagined? So you

went into business for yourself and immediately dived into work.

Doing it, doing it, doing it.

Busy, busy, busy.

Until one day you realized (or maybe not) that you were doing all of the work. You were doing everything you knew how to do, plus a lot more you knew nothing about. Building sweat equity, you thought.

In reality, a technician suffering from an entrepreneurial seizure.

You were just hoping to make a buck in your own practice. And sometimes you did earn a wage. But other times you didn't. You were the one signing the checks all right, but they went to other people.

Does this sound familiar? Is it driving you crazy? Well, relax, because we're going to show you the right way to do it this time.

Read carefully. Be mindful of the moment. You are about to learn the secret you've been waiting for all your working life.

THE PEOPLE LAW

It's critical to know this about the working life of Doctors who own their own practice: *Without people you don't own a practice, you own a job.* And it can be the worst job in the world because you're working for a lunatic! (Nothing personal—we simply have to face the truth if we're ever going to change things.)

Let me state what every Doctor knows: Without people, you're going to have to do it all yourself. Without human help, you're doomed to try to do too much. This isn't a breakthrough idea, but it's amazing how many ignore the truth. They end up knocking themselves out, 12 to 16 hours a day. They try to do more, but less actually gets done.

The load can double you over. Besides what you're used to doing, you may also have to do the books. You'll have to do the organizing. You'll have to do the planning, the buying, the ordering, and the scheduling. And on and on until you're a burned-out husk.

Like painting the Golden Gate Bridge, it's endless. Which makes it beyond the realm of human possibility.

Of course, with others helping you, my Doctor friend, things will start to improve. But only if you truly understand how to engage people in the work you need them to do. When you learn how to do that, when you learn how to replace yourself with other people—people trained in your system—then your practice can really begin to grow. Only then will you begin to experience true freedom yourself.

Doctors often fail to understand that once they surround themselves with people, they've taken on a role other than Doctor. They are now Business Managers. It's not a role most Doctors take seriously.

Typically, Doctors, knowing they need help answering the phone, filing, and so on, go out and find people who can do these things. Once they delegate these duties, however, they rarely spend any time with the hoi polloi. Deep down they feel it's not important *how* these things get done; it's only important that they get done.

They fail to grasp the requirement for a system that makes people their greatest asset rather than their greatest liability. A system so reliable that if Mary dropped dead tomorrow, Judy could do exactly what Mary did.

Here's an important aspect of the People Law:

People allow you to be everywhere you want to be simultaneously, without actually having to be there physically!

People are to a Doctor what a record was to Frank Sinatra. A Sinatra record could be (and still is) played in a million places at the same time, regardless of where Frank was. And every record sale produced royalties for Sinatra (or his estate).

With the help of other people, Sinatra created a quality recording that faithfully replicated his unique talents, then made sure it was marketed, distributed, and the revenue managed.

Your people can do that for you. All *you* need to do is to create a "recording" of your unique talents, your special way of doing business, and then replicate it, market it, distribute it, and manage the revenue. Isn't that what successful businesspeople do? They make a "recording" of their most effective ways of doing business. In this way, they provide a turnkey solution to their own and their patients' problems. A system solution that really works.

Doesn't your practice offer the same potential for you that records did for Frank Sinatra (and now for his heirs)? The ability to produce income without having to go to work every day?

Isn't that what your people could be for you? The means by which your system for practicing medicine could be faithfully replicated?

But first you must have a system. You have to create a unique way of doing business that you can teach to your people, that you can manage faithfully, that you can replicate consistently, just like McDonald's.

Because without such a system, without such a "recording," without a unique way of doing business that really works, all you're left with is people doing their own thing. And that is almost always a recipe for chaos. Rather than guaranteeing consistency, it encourages mistake after mistake after mistake.

And isn't that how the problem started in the first place? People doing whatever *they* perceived they needed to do, regardless of what you wanted? People left to their own devices, with no regard for the costs of their behavior?

In other words, people without a system.

Can you imagine what would have happened to Frank Sinatra if he had followed that example? What if every one of his recordings had been done differently? Imagine a million different versions of "My Way." It's unthinkable.

Would you buy a record like that? What if Frank was having a bad day? What if he had a sore throat?

Please hear this: The People Law is unforgiving. Without a systematic way of doing business, people are more often a liability than an asset. Unless you prepare, you'll find out too late which ones are which.

The People Law says that without a specific system for doing business; without a specific system for recruiting, hiring, and training your people to use that system; and without a specific system for managing and improving your systems, your practice will always be a crapshoot.

Do you want to roll dice with your practice at stake? Unfortunately, that is what most Doctors are doing.

The People Law also says that you can't effectively delegate your responsibilities unless you have something specific to delegate. And that something specific is a way of doing business that works!

Frank Sinatra is gone, but his voice lives on. And someone is still counting his royalties. That's because Sinatra had a system that works.

Do you?

CHAPTER SIX

On the Subject of Employee Doctors

Repetition of actions intensifies the urge to further reiteration and renders their execution easier and better until they come to be performed unconsciously. In this way habits are formed.

THE ACT OF WILL
ROBERT ASSAGIOLI

If you're a sole practitioner—that is, you're selling only yourself—then your company called a practice will never make the leap to a company called a business. The progression from practice to business to enterprise demands that you hire other Doctors to do what you do (or don't do). Contractors call these people Sub-Contractors; we'll call yours Sub-Doctors.

Contractors know that Subs can be a huge problem. It's no less true for Doctors. Until you face this special people problem, your practice will never become a business, and your business will certainly never become an enterprise.

Long ago, God said, "Let there be Doctors. And so they never forget who they are in my creation, let them be damned forever to hire people exactly like themselves." The Sub-Doctors.

Webster's Tenth Collegiate Dictionary defines *sub* as "under, below, secretly; inferior to." We may then define *Sub-Doctor* as an inferior individual or organization contracted to perform part or all of another's contract.

In other words, you, the Doctor, make a conscious decision to hire someone "inferior" to you to fulfill *your* commitment to *your* patient, for which you are ultimately and solely liable!

Why in the world do we do these things to ourselves? Where will this madness lead?

It seems the blind are leading the blind, and the blind are paying others to do it! Talk about an approach doomed to fail at the very outset. It's time to step out of the darkness to see the world as it really is. It's time to do things that work.

SOLVING THE EMPLOYEE DOCTOR PROBLEM

Let's say you're about to hire another Doctor, a Sub-Doctor. Someone who has specific skills: pediatrics, orthopedics, whatever. Of course, it all starts with choosing the right personnel. After all, these are the people to whom you are delegating your responsibility and for whose behavior you are completely liable. Do you really want to leave that choice to chance? Are you that much of a gambler? I doubt it.

If you've never worked with your new Doctor, how do you really know he or she is skilled? For that matter, what does *skilled* mean?

For you to make an intelligent decision about this Sub-Doctor, you must have a working definition of the word *skilled.* Your challenge is to know *exactly* what your expectations are, then to make sure your other Doctors operate with precisely the *same expectations.* Failure here almost assures a breakdown in your relationship.

I want you to write the following on a piece of paper: "By *skilled,* I mean…" Once you create your personal definition, it will become a standard for you and your practice, for your patients, and for your employee Doctors.

A standard, according to *Webster's Tenth,* is something "set up and established by authority as a rule for the measure of quantity, weight, extent, value, or quality."

Thus, your goal is to establish a measure of quality control, a standard of skill, which you will apply to all your Sub-Doctors. More important, you are also setting a standard for the performance of your company.

By creating standards for your selection of other Doctors—standards of skill, performance, integrity, financial stability, and experience—you have begun the powerful process of building a practice that can operate exactly as you expect it to.

By carefully thinking about exactly what you expect, you have already begun to improve your practice.

In this enlightened state, you will see the selection of your Doctors as an opportunity to define what you (1) intend to provide for your patients, (2) expect from your employees, and (3) demand for your life.

Powerful stuff, isn't it? Are you up to it? Are you ready to feel your rising power?

Don't relax quite yet. Defining those standards is only the first step you need to take. The second step is to create a Sub-Doctor Development System.

A Sub-Doctor Development System is an action plan (see Chapter Fourteen) designed to tell you what you are looking for in a Sub-Doctor. It includes the exact Benchmarks, accountabilities, timing of fulfillment, and budget you will assign to the process of looking for Sub-Doctors, identifying them, recruiting them, interviewing them, training them, managing their work, auditing their performance, compensating them, reviewing them regularly, and terminating or rewarding them for their performance. All of these things must be documented if they're going to make any difference to you, or to your Sub-Doctors, or to your managers, or to your bank account.

And then you've got to persist with that system come hell or high water. Just as Ray Kroc did. Just as Walt Disney did. Just as Sam Walton did.

This leads us to another subject, the subject of *estimating.*

CHAPTER SEVEN

On the Subject of Estimating

The leader must give clarity to the vision . . .

so that the independent actions of many

people are powerfully aligned.

HOPE IS NOT A METHOD
GORDON R. SULLIVAN AND MICHAEL V. HARPER

One of the greatest weaknesses of Doctors is accurately estimating how long procedures will take and then scheduling their patients accordingly. *Webster's Tenth New Collegiate Dictionary* defines estimate as "a rough or approximate calculation." Anyone who has visited a Doctor's waiting room knows that those estimates can be rough indeed.

Do you want to see someone who gives you a rough approximation? What if your Doctor gave you a rough approximation of your condition?

The fact is that we can predict many things we

don't typically predict. For example, there are ways to learn the truth about people who come in with the flu or for a physical. Look at the steps of the process. Most of the things you do are standard, so develop a step-by-step system and stick to it.

In my book *The E-Myth Manager,* I raised eyebrows by suggesting that Doctors eliminate the waiting room. Why? You don't need it if you're always on time. Your patients don't have to wait.

What if a Doctor made this promise: "on time, every time, as promised, or we pay for it." Impossible, Doctors cry, because each case is different. We simply can't know how long each patient will take.

Do you follow this? Since Doctors believe they're incapable of knowing how to organize their time, they build a practice based on lack of knowing, lack of control. They build a practice based on estimates.

I once had a Doctor ask me, "What happens when someone comes in with the flu but complains of back trouble in the examination room? How can we deal with something so unexpected? How can we give proper care and stay on schedule?"

My first thought was that it's not being dealt with now. Few Doctors are able to give generously of their time. Ask anyone who's been to a Doctor's office lately. It's chaos.

The solution is interest, attention, analysis. Try detailing what you do at the beginning of an interaction, what you do in the middle, and what you do at the end. How long does each take? In the absence of such detailed, quantified standards, everything ends up being an estimate, and a poor estimate at that.

However, a practice organized around a system has time for proper attention. It's built right into the system.

Too many Doctors have grown accustomed to thinking in terms of estimates without thinking about what the term really means. Is it any wonder most medical practices are in trouble?

Enlightened Doctors, in contrast, banish the word *estimate* from their vocabulary. When it comes to estimating, they just say no!

"But you can never be *exact*," Doctors have told me for years. "Close, maybe. But never exact."

I have a simple answer to that: You have to be! You simply can't afford to be inexact. You can't accept inexactness in yourself or in your practice.

You can't go to work every day believing that your practice, the work you do, and the commitments you make are all too complex and unpredictable to be exact. With a mind-set like that, you're doomed to run a sloppy ship. A ship that will eventually sink and suck you down with it.

This is so easy to avoid. Because sloppiness in thought and action is the root cause of your frustrations.

The solution to those frustrations is clarity. Clarity gives you the ability to set a clear direction, which fuels the momentum you need to grow your practice. Clarity, direction, momentum—all come from insisting on exactness.

But how do you create exactness in a hopelessly inexact world? The answer is, *You discover the exactness in your practice by refusing to do any work that can't be controlled exactly.*

The only other option is to analyze the market, determine where the opportunities are, and then organize your practice to be the exact provider of the services you've chosen to offer.

Two choices, and only two choices: (1) Evaluate your practice and then limit yourself to the tasks you know you can do exactly; or (2) start all over by analyzing the market, identifying the key opportunities in that market, and building a practice that operates exactly.

What you cannot do, what you must refuse to do from this day forward, is to allow yourself to operate with an inexact mind-set. It will lead you to ruin.

Which leads us inexorably back to the word I have been using throughout this book: *systems.*

Who makes estimates? Only Doctors who are unclear about exactly how to do the task in question. Only Doctors whose experience has taught them that if something can go wrong, it will—and to them!

I'm not suggesting that a Systems Solution will guarantee that you always perform exactly as promised. But I am saying that a Systems Solution will faithfully alert you when you're going off track, and will do it before you have to pay a huge price for it.

A STORY OF PATIENT DISSATISFACTION

Here's a story that is disturbingly typical of what millions of people face at the Doctor's office. This happened to Barbara Berg, the mother of one of my employees.

"I had a 2:00 appointment to see an ENT specialist about this chronic nasal congestion I have," she told me. "Being a good scout, I arrived at the doctor's office at 1:45. The girl at the front desk had me sign in and then told me to take a seat. 'The Doctor will be with you in just a few minutes,' she cooed.

"Well, I didn't exactly believe that, but I try to be optimistic. Sitting in the large waiting room, I read old magazines and glanced at my fellow patients, idly wondering what ailed them.

"After ten minutes, they called my name, but they only wanted me to sign another paper. Back in my seat, it occurred to me that the problem begins with the name—the *waiting room*. After all, if you have a waiting room, you're going to use it.

"After twenty minutes, they called my name again. Now I felt special, chosen, but it was just time to go into the next waiting room, the little waiting room. Once there, I was told to put on one of those charming, drafty hospital gowns. I complied, even though my problem—chronic nasal congestion—didn't seem to require a complete change of clothes. The nurse took my weight, temperature, and blood pressure, assured me the doctor would be right along, and then left me alone.

"And there I sat—for one solid hour! Finally, out of magazines, with blood pressure soaring off the charts, I opened the door and said to no one in particular: 'I'm going to get dressed and leave.'

"A nurse came jogging in, full of apologies and promises of the doctor's imminent arrival. And, in fact, he soon did arrive. He was brusque but not unfriendly. After asking me a couple of questions, he took his tool and looked up my nose. A moment later, he flatly announced that I had a slightly deviated septum. 'It's nothing serious,' he assured me."

I asked Barbara if the Doctor or anyone in his office ever apologized for his tardiness.

"No one explained. No one apologized," she said.

Now, why couldn't that Doctor run his practice on time? Imagine his patients' soaring satisfaction if he had. What would it have taken? Just a simple system. And a determination to abandon rough estimates.

A simple system would meet the needs of hundreds of patients. Who wouldn't want to do business with a Doctor like that?

In short, with a Systems Solution in place, your need to estimate will be a thing of the past, both because you have organized your practice to anticipate mistakes and because you have put into place the system to do something about those mistakes before they blow up.

There's this, too: To make a Promise you intend to keep places a burden on you and your managers to dig deeply into how you intend to keep it. Such a burden will transform your intentions and boost your attention to detail.

With the Promise will come dedication. With dedication will come integrity. With integrity will come consistency. With consistency will come results you can count on. And results you can count on mean that you get exactly what you hoped for at the outset of your practice: the true pride of ownership that every Doctor should experience.

And no more patients grousing about having to wait an hour.

This brings us to the subject of *patients*. Who are they? Why do they come to you? How can you identify yours? And who *should* your patients be?

CHAPTER EIGHT

On the Subject of Patients

Ordinary failures in work are an inevitable part
of the descent of the spirit into human limitation.

CARE OF THE SOUL
THOMAS MOORE

My friend, Dr. Kivett, a cosmetic surgeon in Santa Rosa, California, believes that patients have helped to knock Doctors off their pedestal. "In cosmetic surgery, the average patient waits 13 minutes. A few years ago, it was 26 minutes. Patients have become more demanding. After a 20-minute wait, a wealthy woman recently told me indignantly, 'I could've been doing other things.'"

What's more, it's a rare patient who shows any appreciation for what a Doctor has to go through to do the job as promised. Don't they always think the price is too high? And don't they focus on problems, broken promises, and the mistakes they think you make, rather than all the times you bend over backward to give them what they need?

Do you ever hear other Doctors voice these complaints? More to the point, have you ever voiced them, even to yourself? Well, you're not alone. I have yet to meet a Doctor who doesn't suffer from a strong case of patient confusion.

Patient confusion is about:

- What your patient really wants

- How to communicate with your patient effectively

- How to deal with your patient's dissatisfaction

- How to keep your patient truly happy

HOW TO KEEP YOUR PATIENT HAPPY

How do you keep your patient happy? Very simple . . . just keep your promise! And make sure your patient *knows* you kept your promise every step of the way.

In short, giving your patients what they think they want is the key to keeping them (or anyone else, for that matter) really happy. Says Dr. Kivett: "Doctors who treat their patients unlike other businesses treat their customers are missing the point. Patients are like any other kind of consumers."

At E-Myth, we recognize that, and we've created the antidote: the Client Fulfillment System. It's the step-by-step process by which you do the task you've contracted to do and deliver what you've promised—on time, every time.

But what happens when your patient is *not* happy? What happens when you've done everything I've mentioned here and your patient is still dissatisfied?

HOW TO DEAL WITH PATIENT DISSATISFACTION

If you have hit each step to this point, patient dissatisfaction will be rare. But dissatisfactions will occur. Here's what to do about them:

1. **Always listen to what your patients are saying. And never interrupt while they're saying it.**

2. **After you're sure you've heard all of your patient's complaint, make absolutely certain you understand what she said: "Can I repeat what you've just told me, Mrs. Jones, to make absolutely certain I understand you?"**

3. **Secure your patient's acknowledgment that you have heard her complaint accurately.**

4. **Apologize for whatever it is your patient thinks you did that dissatisfied her . . . even if you didn't do it!**

5. After your patient has acknowledged your apology, ask her exactly what would make her happy.

6. Repeat what your patient told you that it would take to make her happy, and get her acknowledgment that you have heard correctly.

7. If at all possible, give your patient exactly what she has asked for.

But what if your Patient wants something completely unreasonable? If you've followed my recommendations to the letter, what your patient asks for will seldom seem unreasonable.

In short, *it's all up to you.* No mystery. No magic. Just a systematic process for shaping your practice's future. But you must have the passion to pursue the process. And you must be absolutely clear about every aspect of it.

Until you know your patients as well as you know yourself.

Until all your complaints about patients are a thing of the past.

Until you accept the undeniable fact that patient acquisition and patient satisfaction are more science than art.

But unless you're willing to grow your practice, you better not follow any of these recommendations. Because it will grow.

This brings us to the subject of *growth.*

CHAPTER NINE

On the Subject of Growth

First of all, we have to understand that the present
does not exist in any particularly convincing way.
We are always concerned with seeing what
has just happened, not what is happening.

THE WAY TO BE FREE
J. G. BENNETT

The rule of business growth says that every business, like every child, is destined to grow! Needs to grow. Is determined to grow.

Once you've created your business, once you've shaped the idea of it, the most natural thing for it to do is to . . . *grow!* And if you stop it from growing, it will die.

Once a Doctor has started a practice, it's his or her job to help it grow. To nurture it and support it in every way. To infuse it with:

- Purpose

- Passion

- Will

- Belief

- Personality

- Method

As your practice grows, it naturally changes. And as it changes from a little practice to something much bigger, you will begin to feel out of control. That's because you *are* out of control!

Your practice has exceeded your know-how, sprinted right past you, and now it's taunting you to keep up. That leaves two choices: (1) Grow as big as your practice demands, or (2) try to hold your practice at its present level. At the level you feel most comfortable.

Sadly, most Doctors do the latter. They try to keep their practice small, within their comfort zone. Doing what they know how to do, what they feel most comfortable doing. It's called playing it safe.

But as the practice grows, the number, scale, and complexity of tasks will grow, too, until they threaten to overwhelm the Doctor. More people are needed. More technology. More money. Everything seems to be happening at the same time. A hundred balls are in the air at once.

As I've said throughout this book, *most Doctors are not entrepreneurs; they are not truly businesspeople but technicians suffering from an entrepreneurial seizure.* Their philosophy of coping with the workload can be summarized as "Just do it." In other words, thoughtless action instead of figuring out how to do things through other people using innovative systems to produce consistent results.

Given most Doctors' inclination to be the master juggler in their practice, it's not surprising that as complexity increases, as work expands beyond their ability to do it, as money becomes more elusive, they are just holding on, desperately juggling more and more balls. In the end, most collapse under the strain.

You can't expect your practice to stand still. You can't expect your practice to stay small. A practice that stays small and depends on you to do everything isn't a practice—it's a job! And you're working for a lunatic.

Yes, just like your children, your practice must be allowed to grow, to flourish, to change, to become more than it is. In this way, it will match your vision.

Do you feel the excitement? You should. After all, you know what your practice *is* but not what it *can be.*

It's either going to grow or die. The choice is yours, but it is a choice that must be made. For if you sit back and wait for change to overtake you, you will always have to answer no to this question: Are you ready?

This brings us to the subject of *change.*

CHAPTER TEN

On the Subject of Change

Everything here shakes

shivers

bends

blasts

in fierce gamble

CHARLES BUKOWSKI

So your practice is growing. That means, of course, that it's also changing, which means it's driving you and everyone in your life crazy.

That's because, to most people, change is a diabolical thing. Tell most people they've got to change, and they will crawl into a shell. Nothing threatens their existence more than change. Nothing cements their resistance more than change. Nothing.

Yet for the past 30 years, that's exactly what I've

been proposing to small business owners: the need to change. Not for the sake of change but for the sake of their lives.

I've talked to countless small practitioners whose hopes weren't being realized through their practice; whose lives were consumed by work; who slaved increasingly longer hours for decreasing pay; whose dissatisfaction grew as their enjoyment shriveled; whose practice had become the worst job in the world; whose money was out of control; whose employees were a source of never-ending hassles, just like their patients, their bank, and, increasingly, even their family.

More and more, these Doctors spent their time alone, dreading the unknown, anxious about the future. And even when they were with people, they didn't know how to relax. Their mind was always on the job. They were distracted by work, by the thought of work. By the fear of falling behind.

And yet, when confronted with their condition and offered an alternative, most of these same Doctors strenuously resisted. They assumed that if there were a better way of doing business, they already would have figured it out. They derived comfort from knowing what they believed they already knew. They accepted the limitations of being a Doctor; the limitations of what they should expect from patients, employees, other Doctors, even family and friends.

In short, most Doctors I've met over the years

would rather live with the frustrations they already have than risk enduring new frustrations.

Isn't that true of most people you know? Rather than opening up to the infinite number of possibilities life offers, they prefer to impose limits, to erect barriers, to shut their life down to respectable limits. And, after all, isn't that the most reasonable way to live?

I think not. I think we must learn to let go. I think that if we fail to embrace change, it will inevitably destroy us.

Conversely, by opening ourselves to change, we give our practice the opportunity to get the most from our talents.

Let me share with you an original way to think about change, about life, about who we are and what we do. About the stunning notion of expansion and contraction.

"Our salvation," a wise man once said, "is to allow." That is, to be open, to let go of our beliefs, to change. Only then can we move from a point of view to a viewing point.

CONTRACTION VERSUS EXPANSION

That man was Thaddeus Golas, the author of a small, powerful book entitled *The Lazy Man's Guide to Enlightenment* (Seed Center, 1971).

Among the many inspirational things he said was this compelling idea:

The basic function of each being is expanding and contracting. Expanded beings are permeative; contracted beings are dense and impermeative. Therefore each of us, alone or in combination, may appear as space, energy, or mass, depending on the ration of expansion to contraction chosen, and what kind of vibrations each of us expresses by alternating expansion and contraction. Each being controls his own vibrations.

In other words, Golas tells us that the entire mystery of life can be summed up in two words: *expansion* and *contraction.* He continues:

We experience expansion as awareness, comprehension, understanding, or whatever we wish to call it.

When we are completely expanded, we have a feeling of total awareness, of being one with all life.

At that level we have no resistance to any vibrations or interactions with other beings. It is timeless bliss, with unlimited choice of consciousness, perception, and feeling.

On the other hand, when a (human) being is totally contracted, he is a mass particle, completely imploded.

To the degree that he is contracted, a being is unable to be in the same space with others, so con-

traction is felt as fear, pain, unconsciousness, igno-
rance, hatred, evil, and a whole host of strange feel-
ings.

At an extreme (of contraction), a human being
has the feeling of being completely insane, of
resisting everyone and everything, of being
unable to choose the content of his conscious-
ness.

Of course, these are just the feelings appropri-
ate to mass vibration levels, and he can get out of
them at any time by expanding, by letting go of all
resistance to what he thinks, sees, or feels.

Stay with me here. Because what Golas says is profoundly important. When you're feeling oppressed,
overwhelmed, exhausted by more than you can control—contracted, as Golas puts it—you can change
your state to one of expansion.

According to Golas, the more contracted we are,
the more threatened by change; the more expanded
we are, the more open to change.

In our most enlightened—that is, open—state,
change is as welcome as nonchange. Everything is
perceived as a part of ourselves. There is no inside or
outside. Everything is one thing. Our sense of isola-
tion is transformed to a feeling of ease, of light, of
joyful relationship with everything.

As infants, we didn't even think of change in the
same way, because we lived those first days in an

unthreatened state. Insensitive to the threat of loss, most young children are only aware of *what is.* Change is simply another form of *what is.* Change just *is.*

In our most contracted—that is, closed—state, however, change is the most extreme threat. If the known is what I have, then the unknown must be what threatens to take away what I have. For those in a closed state, change elicits fear of the unknown. It's like being between trapezes.

To the fearful, change is threatening because things may get worse.

To the hopeful, change is encouraging because things may get better.

To the confident, change is inspiring because the challenge exists to improve things.

If you are fearful, you see difficulties in every opportunity. If you are fear-free, you see opportunities in every difficulty.

Fear protects what I have from being taken away. But it also disconnects me from the rest of the world. That is, fear keeps me separate and alone.

Here's the exciting part of Golas's message: With this new understanding of contraction and expansion, we can become completely attuned to where we are at all times.

If I am afraid, suspicious, skeptical, and resistant, I am in a contracted state. If I am joyful, open, interested, and willing, I am in an expanded state. Just knowing this puts me on an expanded path. Always remembering this, Golas says, brings enlightenment, which opens me even more.

Such openness gives me the ability to freely access my options. And taking advantage of options is the best part of change. Just as there are infinite ways to greet a patient, there are infinite ways to run your practice. According to Theodore Golas, your most exciting option is to be open to all of them.

Because your life is lived on a continuum between the most contracted and most expanded—the most closed and most open—states, change is best understood as the movement along that continuum.

Most small business owners I've met see change as a thing-in-itself, as something that just happens to them. Most experience change as a threat. Whenever change shows up at the door, they quickly slam it. Many bolt the door and pile up the furniture. Some even run for their gun.

Few of them understand that change isn't a thing-in-itself but rather the manifestation of many things. Think of it as the revelation of all possibilities. Think of it as the ability at any moment to sacrifice what we are for what we could become.

Change can either challenge us or threaten us. It's our choice. Our attitude toward change can either pave the way to success or throw up a roadblock.

Change is where opportunity lives. Without

change we would stay exactly as we are. The universe would be frozen still. Time would end.

At any given moment, we are somewhere on the path between a contracted and expanded state. Most of us are somewhere between the two extremes, neither totally closed nor totally open.

According to Golas, change is our movement from our place in the middle toward one of the two ends.

Do you want to move toward contraction or enlightenment? Without change, you are hopelessly stuck with what you've got.

Without Change:

- We have no hope

- We cannot know true joy

- We will not get better

- We will continue to focus exclusively on what we have and the threat of losing it

All of this negativity contracts us even more, until, at the extreme closed end of the spectrum, we become a black hole so dense that no light can get in or out.

Sadly, the harder we try to hold on to what we've got, the less able we are to do it. So we try still harder, which eventually drags us even deeper into the black hole of contraction.

Are you like that? Do you know anybody who is?

*　　*　　*

Think of change as the movement between where we are and where we're not. That leaves only two directions for change: either moving forward or slipping backward. We either become more contracted or more expanded.

The next step is to link change to how we feel: If we feel afraid, change is dragging us backward. If we feel open, change is pushing us forward.

Change is not a thing-in-itself but a movement of our consciousness. By tuning in, by paying attention, we get clues to the state of our being.

Change, then, is not an outcome or something to be acquired. Change is a shift of our consciousness, of our being, of our humanity, of our attention, of our relationship with all other beings in the universe.

We are either "more in relationship," or "less in relationship." Change is the movement in either of those directions. The exciting part is that *we possess the ability to decide which way we go . . . and to know in the moment which way we're moving.*

Closed, open. . . . Open, closed. Two directions in the universe. The choice is yours.

Do you sense the profound opportunity available here?

Enlightenment is not reserved for the sainted. Rather, it comes to us as we become more sensitive to ourselves. Eventually, we become our own guides, alerting ourselves to our state, moment by moment: *Open . . . Closed . . . Open . . . Closed.*

Listen to your inner voice, your ally, and feel what it's like to be open and closed. Experience the instant of choice in both directions.

You will feel the awareness growing. It may be only a flash at first, so be alert. This feeling is accessible, but only if you avoid the black hole of contraction.

Are you totally contracted? It's doubtful. The fact that you're still reading this book suggests that you're moving in the opposite direction.

You're more like a running back seeking the open field. You can see opportunity gleaming in the distance. In the open direction.

Understand, I'm not saying that change itself is a point on the path; rather, it's the all-important movement.

Change is *in you,* not *out there.*

What path are you on? The path of Liberation? Or the path of Crystallization?

As we know, change can be for the better or for the worse.

If change is happening *inside* of you, it is for the worse only if you remain closed to it. The key, then, is your attitude—your acceptance or rejection of change. For change can be for the better only if you accept it. And it will certainly be for the worse if you don't.

Remember, change is nothing in itself. Without you, change doesn't exist. Change is happening inside of each of us, giving us clues to where we are at any point in time.

Rejoice in change, for it's a sign you're alive.

Are we open? Are we closed? If we're open, good things are bound to happen. If we're closed, things will only get worse.

According to Golas, it's as simple as that. Whatever happens defines where we are. *How* we are is *where* we are. It cannot be any other way.

For change is Life.

Charles Darwin wrote, "It is not the strongest of the species that survive, nor the most intelligent, but the one that proves itself most responsive to change."

The growth of your medical practice, then, is its change. Your role is to go with it, to be with it, to share the joy, embrace the opportunities, meet the challenges, learn the lessons.

Remember, there are three kinds of people: (1) those who make things happen, (2) those who let things happen, and (3) those who wonder what the hell happened. The people who make things happen are masters of change. The other two are its victims.

Which type are you?

If all this is going to mean anything to the life of your practice, you have to know when you're going to leave it. At what point in your practice's rise from where it is now to where it can ultimately grow are you going to sell it? Because if you don't have a clear picture of when you want out, your practice is the master of your destiny, not the reverse. As we stated in Chapter Two, the most valuable form of money is Equity, and unless your business vision includes your Equity and how you will use it to your advantage, you will be forever consumed by your practice.

Your practice is potentially the best friend you ever had. It is your practice's nature to serve you, so let it. However, if you are not a wise steward, if you do not tell your practice what you expect from it, it will run rampant, abuse you, use you, and confuse you.

Change. Growth. Equity.

Focus on the point in the future when you will take leave of your practice. Now reconsider your goals in that context. Be specific. Skipping this step is like tiptoeing through earthquake country.

Who knows where the fault lies waiting?

And now on to the subject of *time*.

CHAPTER ELEVEN

On the Subject of Time

I would if I could stand on a busy corner,
hat in hand, and beg people to throw
me all their wasted hours.

BERNARD BERENSON

'm running out of time!" Doctors often lament.
"I've got to learn how to manage my time more
carefully!"

Of course, they see no real solution to this problem. They're just worrying the subject to death.
Singing the Doctor's Blues.

Some make a real effort to control time. Maybe
they go to time management classes, or faithfully try
to record their activities during every hour of the day.

But it's hopeless. Even when Doctors work
harder, even when they keep precise records of their
time, there's always a shortage of it. It's as if they're

looking at a square clock in a round universe. Something doesn't fit. The result: The Doctor is constantly chasing work, money, life.

And the reason is simple. The Doctor doesn't see time for what it really is. He thinks of time with a small t rather than Time with a capital T.

Yet Time is simply another word for *your life.* It's your ultimate asset, your gift at birth—and you can spend it any way you want. Do you know how you want to spend it? Do you have a plan?

How do *you* deal with Time? Are you even conscious of it? If you are, I bet you are constantly locked into either the future or the past. Relying on either memory or imagination.

Do you recognize these voices? "Once I get through this, I can have a drink . . . go on vacation . . . retire." "I remember when I was young and medicine was satisfying."

As you go to bed at 10 P.M., are you thinking about waking up at 7 A.M. so that you can get to the office by 8 A.M. so that you can go to lunch by noon, because Dr. Butane will be there at 2 P.M. and you've got that colonoscopy at 4 P.M. . . . ?

Most of us are prisoners of the future or the past. While pinballing between the two, we miss the richest moments of our life—the present. Trapped forever in memory or imagination, we are strangers to the here and now. Our future is nothing more than an extension of our past, and the present is merely the background.

It's sobering to think that right now each of us is at a precise spot somewhere between the beginning of our Time (our birth) and the end of our Time (our death).

No wonder everyone frets about Time. What really terrifies us is *we're using up our life and we can't stop it.*

It feels as if we're plummeting toward the end with nothing to break our free fall. Time is out of control! Understandably, this is horrifying, mostly because the real issue is not time with a small t but Death with a big D.

We are trying to put Time in a different perspective—all the while pretending we can manage it! We talk about Time as though it were something other than what it is. "Time is Money," we announce, as though that explains it.

But what every Doctor should know is that Time is life. And Time ends! Life ends!

The big, walloping, unresolvable problem is that *we don't know how much Time we have left!*

Do you feel the fear? Do you want to get over it?

Let's look at Time more seriously.

To fully grasp Time with a capital T, you have to ask the Big Question: *How do I wish to spend the rest of my Time?*

Because I can assure you that if you don't ask that Big Question with a big Q, you'll forever be assailed by the little questions. You'll shrink the whole of your life to *this time* and *next time* and the *last time*—all the while wondering, *What time is it?*

It's like running around the deck of a sinking ship worrying about where you left the keys to your cabin.

You must accept that you have only so much Time, that you're using up that Time second by precious second. And that your Time, your life, is the most valuable asset you have. Of course, you can use your Time any way you want. But unless you choose to use it as richly, as rewardingly, as excitingly, as intelligently, as *intentionally* as possible, you'll squander it and fail to appreciate it.

Indeed, if you are oblivious to the value of your Time, you'll commit the single greatest sin: You will live your life unconscious of its passing you by.

Until you deal with Time with a capital T, you'll worry about time with a small t until you have no Time—or life—left. Then your Time will be history—along with your life.

Scary, isn't it?

I can anticipate the question: If Time is the problem, why not just book fewer patients? Well, that's certainly an option, but probably not necessary. I know a veterinarian with a small practice whose Doctors see four times as many patients as the average, yet they don't work long hours. How is it possible? He has a system. Roughly 50 percent of what needs to be communicated to patients is "downloaded" to office staff.

By using this expert system, the kids can do everything the vet would do that isn't Doctor dependent.

BE VERSUS DO

Remember when we all asked, "What do I want to *be* when I grow up?" It was one of our biggest concerns as children.

But notice that the question isn't, "What do I want to *do* when I grow up?"

Shakespeare wrote, "To be or not to be." Not, "To do or not to do."

But when you grow up, people always ask you, "What do you *do?*" How did the question change from *being* to *doing?* How did we miss the critical distinction between the two? After all, *being* is qualitatively different from *doing.*

Even as children, we sensed the distinction. The real question we were asking was not what we would end up *doing* but who we would *be.*

We were talking about a *life* choice, not a *work* choice. We instinctively saw it as a matter of how we spend our Time, not what we do *in* time.

Look to children for guidance. I believe that as children we instinctively saw Time as life and tried to use it wisely. As children, we wanted to make a life choice, not a work choice. As children, we didn't know—or care—that work had to be done on time, on budget.

Until you see Time for what it really is—your life span—you will always ask the wrong question. Until you embrace the whole of your Time and shape it accordingly, you will never be able to fully appreciate the moment. Until you fully appreciate every second that comprises Time, you will never be sufficiently motivated to live those seconds fully. Until you're sufficiently motivated to live those seconds fully, you will never see fit to change the way you are. You will never take the quality and sanctity of Time seriously.

Unless you take the sanctity of Time seriously, you will continue to struggle to catch up with something behind you. Your frustrations will mount as you try to snatch the second that just whisked by.

If you constantly fret about time with a small t, then big-T Time will blow right past you. And you'll miss the whole point, the real truth about Time: You can't manage it; you never could. You can only *live* it.

And so that leaves you with these questions: How do I live my life? How do I give significance to it? How can I be here now in this moment?

CHAPTER TWELVE

On the Subject of Work

There's so much talk about the system.

And so little understanding.

ZEN AND THE ART OF MOTORCYCLE MAINTENANCE
ROBERT M. PIRSIG

In the business world, as the saying goes, the entrepreneur knows something about everything, the technician knows everything about something, and the switchboard operator just knows everything.

In a medical practice, Doctors see their natural work as the work of the technician. The Supreme Technician. Often to the exclusion of everything else.

After all, Doctors get zero preparation working as a manager and spend no time thinking as an entrepreneur. They're just doing it, doing it, doing it.

At the same time, they want everything—freedom, respect, money. Most of all, they want to rid themselves of meddling bosses and start their own practice. That way they can be their own boss and take home all the money. These Doctors are in the throes of an entrepreneurial seizure.

Doctors who have been praised for their bedside manner or medical knowledge believe they have what it takes to run a medical practice. It's not unlike the plumber who becomes a contractor because he's a great plumber. He knows how to be a plumber, but it doesn't necessarily follow that he knows how to build a practice that does this work. It's the same for a Doctor.

I'm not saying that the Doctor can't practice medicine anymore, that he or she can't be a Doctor. But she has to create a separate sense of self, apart from being the chief. She has to jump out of her body and look at it from afar so that she can begin to see her relationship to the rest of the office. She has to develop a better understanding of what she is supposed to do not only as a Doctor but as a manager and entrepreneur. To fail to do this creates enormous conflict in the office.

Doctors must then organize work differently. They can't ignore it. It's a mistake to think *that's your job. That's what I'm paying you for.* Doctors have to accept the responsibility for coordinating the effort.

Lacking that coordination, there is no connection between the needs of the business side and the needs of the medical side. This fragmentation inevitably leads to further conflict. Businessperson versus medical person. And everyone else is simply chattel. The result? The nurses hate the system. The Doctor hates the nurses; the nurses hate the Doctor. No one respects anyone else.

The Doctor can't bear that he's not getting the adulation he should be getting for being who he is— the next best thing to God. Meanwhile, everybody else thinks the Doctor is out of touch. But even if they have the temerity to say so, the Doctor can't hear them.

Do you see the trap? Doctors have spent enormous amounts of time and money getting through school, becoming a star. Why, then, they mistakenly think, should they have to attend to such mundane tasks?

More than any other subject, work is the cause of obsessive-compulsive behavior by Doctors.

Work. You've got to do it every single day.

Work. If you fall behind, you'll pay for it.

Work. There's either too much or not enough.

So many Doctors describe work as what they do when they are busy. Some discriminate between the work *they could be doing* as Doctors and the work *they should be doing* as Doctors.

But according to The E-Myth, they're exactly the same thing. The work you *could* do and the work you *should* do as a Doctor are identical. Let me explain.

STRATEGIC VERSUS TACTICAL WORK

Doctors can do only two kinds of work: Strategic Work and Tactical Work.

Tactical Work is easier to understand, because it's what almost every Doctor does almost every minute of every hour of every day. It's called getting the job done. It's called doing business.

Tactical Work includes filing, billing, answering the telephone, going to the bank, and seeing patients.

The E-Myth says that Tactical Work is all the work Doctors find themselves doing in a medical practice to *avoid* doing the Strategic Work.

"I'm too busy," most Doctors will tell you.

"How come nothing goes right unless I do it myself?" they complain in frustration.

Doctors say these things when they're up to their ears in Tactical Work. But most Doctors don't understand that if they had done more Strategic Work, they would have less Tactical Work to do.

Doctors are doing Strategic Work when they ask the following questions:

- Why am I a Doctor?

- What will my practice look like when it's done?

- What must my practice look, act, and feel like in order to compete successfully?

- What are the Key Indicators of my practice?

Please note that I said Doctors *ask* these questions when they are doing Strategic Work. I didn't say these are the questions they necessarily *answer.*

That is the fundamental difference between Strategic Work and Tactical Work. Tactical Work is all about *answers:* How to do this. How to do that.

Strategic Work, in contrast, is all about *questions:* What practice are we really in? Why are we in that practice? Who specifically is our practice determined to serve? When will I sell this practice? How and where will this practice be doing business when I sell it? And so forth.

Not that Strategic Questions don't have answers. Doctors who commonly ask Strategic Questions know that once they ask such a question, they're already on their way to *envisioning* the answer. Within the Strategic Question resides the answer. Question and answer are part of a whole. You can't find the right answer until you've asked the right question.

Tactical Work is much easier, because the question is always more obvious. In fact, you don't ask the Tactical Question; instead, the question arises from a result you need to get or a problem you need to solve. Billing an insurance company is Tactical Work. Filling out a medical report is Tactical Work. Firing an employee is Tactical Work. Seeing a patient is Tactical Work.

Tactical Work is the stuff you do every day in your practice. Strategic Work is the stuff you plan to do to create an exceptional business.

In Tactical Work, the question comes from *out there* rather than *in here.* The Tactical Question is about something *outside* of you, whereas the Strategic Question is about something *inside* of you.

The Tactical Question is about something you *need* to do, whereas the Strategic Question is about something you *want* to do. Want versus Need.

If Tactical Work consumes you:

- You are always reacting to something outside of you

- Your practice runs you; you don't run it

- The job runs you; you don't run it

- Your employees run you; you don't run them

- Your life runs you; you don't run your life

You must understand that the more Strategic Work you do, the more intentional your decisions, your practice, and your life become. *Intention* is the byword of Strategic Work.

Everything on the outside begins to serve you, to serve your vision, rather than forcing you to serve it. Everything you *need* to do is congruent with what you *want* to do. It means you have a vision, an aim, a purpose, a strategy, an *envisioned* result.

Strategic Work is the work you do to *design* your practice, to design your life.

Tactical Work is the work you do to *implement* the design created by Strategic Work.

Without Strategic Work, there is no design. Without Strategic Work, all that's left is keeping busy.

Let's look at someone who learned the important difference between Strategic Work and Tactical Work. Let's look at the story of Dr. Sandy.

CHAPTER THIRTEEN

The Story of Dr. Sandy

I know now that it is better to face a fearful situation than to ignore
it, to accept the fact that it's all right to be fearful.

ZEN IN THE MARTIAL ARTS
JOE HYAMS

Now let's meet someone who is the embodiment of the principles we've discussed. Dr. Sandy Blake owned his own medical practice. On his staff were three administrative people, including an administrative manager. There were also four medical assistants, two practitioners, and an office manager.

Most people would call Dr. Sandy's practice successful. His people were busy; the waiting room was packed; the Doctor's schedule was maxed out.

Of course, such success came with a price. Stacks of file folders overflowed onto the floor; invoices went out late; people who telephoned spent several minutes on hold.

Meanwhile, the practice continued to grow. As it did, Dr. Sandy lost much of what had originally drawn people to him. The waiting room was often standing room only. You could expect to wait an average of 23 minutes before being ushered into the examination room. There, a medical assistant would take your temperature and blood pressure and ask you to strip down to the essentials. Then the medical assistant would leave and you would wait. There was no telling for how long.

Finally, Dr. Sandy or one of his practitioners would enter, looking harried and preoccupied. After a glance at your chart and a glance at you, the Doctor would ask, "How ya feeling?" It was irritating to hear that question over and over. The Doctor's sheer ignorance of your condition was rankling. It showed such lack of respect for, or even acknowledgment of, the value of your time.

It hadn't always been that way. When I first began to work with Dr. Sandy on the transformation of his practice, I asked many of his longtime patients what it had been like in the early days. With more than a touch of nostalgia, they recalled a time when Dr. Sandy's offices were freshly painted and attractively decorated, clean, and well lighted. In those halcyon days, the medical people had made them feel well cared for, even special.

Now, Dr. Sandy's exuberance—the trait that had drawn so many to his doors—was dimmed. Smiles and convivial chitchat had been replaced by the steady hum of office equipment and no-nonsense business talk.

The condition I describe here is not unique; in fact, it is quite common. Dr. Sandy is exceptional in that he realized the error of his ways. Before it was too late, he had an epiphany: In order to have the kind of practice that both patients and employees loved, he would have to reinvent the experience so that it could be repeated every day.

When Dr. Sandy had that realization, everything changed. Further leaps of understanding were now possible.

He came to understand the difference between having an experience and creating one. Between working *on* his practice and working *in* his practice. With this came an understanding of the power of marketing.

At the core of his medical practice, Dr. Sandy eventually discovered a promise that would forever alter not only his own perceptions of the practice of medicine but the perceptions of his employees and patients. And that promise was, *We will be on time, every time, exactly as promised. Or we will pay for your visit!*

This promise sent an implicit but powerful message to his patients: *We made a terrible mistake here. We made appointments with you and then failed to respect that commitment. We know that makes you angry. We compromised the efficiency of our practice, the joy of our practice, the vitality of our practice, the effectiveness of our practice. No more!*

Of course, no one in the practice, including Dr. Sandy himself, had the slightest idea how they were going to keep that promise. Because no one in the profession had ever made such a promise before.

For Dr. Sandy, it was a leap of faith. He believed that by merely making such a promise, he would begin to reenergize his practice. By focusing on the patients—who they were, what they wanted—Dr. Sandy remembered why he had entered the medical profession in the first place.

He found out about his patients by . . . *asking them.* He held a drawing and gave away prizes. To enter, a patient merely had to fill out a questionnaire. Dr. Sandy asked his patients which colors they preferred, which shapes, which words. Then he studied these data and redesigned his offices accordingly.

Dr. Sandy forced employees to think—really think—about the ways they conducted business. He challenged them to find ways to conduct it more responsibly, more efficiently. He challenged them to find ways to keep their promise.

He instilled a marketing mind-set in all his people. He made them realize it was not enough to simply become more efficient at what they do; they also had to become stunningly more effective in a way that distinguished their organization from the competition. Achieving this goal demanded the attention and commitment of everyone.

It demanded everyone to constantly ask: *What would a world-class practice like ours look like, feel like, act like, perform like?*

The transformation of Dr. Sandy's practice was staggering. He implemented systems to teach the staff how to automate the practice, how to clean up filings and streamline billings, and how to meet the patients in a more joyful way.

From that one promise followed many more promises that Dr. Sandy's office made and kept—promises no one had ever thought of before.

In the process of rethinking his practice, Dr. Sandy asked the key questions—the same questions you should ask:

- What's driving my patients—my customers—crazy?

- How am I making it difficult/impossible for my people to get the results for which they're being held accountable?

- How could I make their work, and therefore their lives, easier?

You will find that answering these questions is less about solving problems than seizing opportunities. Once you discover the answers, you must ask: *How quickly can I implement the necessary changes?*

Dr. Sandy ultimately learned that although most people equate marketing with promotion or advertising, it is nothing more—or less—than attraction. An offer you can't refuse is the essence of attraction. And attraction is the essence of great marketing.

Marketing done well is a commitment to provide your patients, your employees, and yourself with a business experience that is life sustaining, with a relationship that is renewing, and with a process that says to everyone, *You matter.*

Marketing communicates your promise, but it also focuses on the way your practice delivers that promise.

True marketing demands that you understand that your entire organization is in fact the product being offered for sale. That is, marketing is not simply words, pictures, commercials, and brochures; it is your entire system geared up to deliver your promise.

An E-Myth organization doesn't just *do* marketing; it *is* marketing.

CHAPTER FOURTEEN

On the Subject of Taking Action

Today is the first day of the rest of your life.

ANONYMOUS

So, it's time to get started, time to take action. Time to stop thinking about the old practice (OldCo) and start thinking about the new practice (NewCo). It's not a matter of coming up with better practices; it's about reinventing the practice of medicine.

And the Doctor has to take personal responsibility for it.

That means Doctors have to be interested. They cannot abdicate accountability for the practice of medicine, the administration of medicine, or the finance of medicine.

Although the goal is to create systems into which Doctors can plug reasonably competent people—

systems that allow the practice to run without them—Doctors must take responsibility for that happening.

I can hear the chorus: "But we're Doctors. We shouldn't have to know about this." Of course, you should.

All too often, Doctors take no responsibility for the business of medicine but instead delegate tasks without any understanding of what it takes to do them; without any interest in what their people are actually doing; without any sense of what it feels like to be at the front counter when a patient comes in and has to wait 45 minutes; and without any appreciation for the entity that is creating their livelihood.

Doctors can open the portals of change in an instant. All you have to do is say, "I don't want to do it that way anymore." Saying it will begin to set you free—even though you don't yet understand what the practice will look like after it's been reinvented.

This demands an intentional leap from the known into the unknown. It further demands that you live there—in the unknown—for a while. It means discarding the past, everything you once believed to be true.

Think of it as soaring rather than plunging.

You should now be clear about the need to first organize your thoughts, then your business. Because the organization of your thoughts is the foundation for the organization of your business.

If we try to organize our business without organizing our thoughts, we will fail to attack the problem.

Organization is not simply Time Management. Nor is it People Management. Nor is it tidying up desks or alphabetizing files. Organization is first, last, and always cleaning up the mess of our minds.

By learning how to *think* about the practice of medicine, by learning how to *think* about our priorities, and by learning how to *think* about our lives, we prepare ourselves to do righteous battle with the forces of failure.

Right Thinking leads to Right Action—and now is the time to take action. Because it is only through action that we can translate thoughts into movement in the real world, and, in the process, find fulfillment.

So, first we *think* about what we want to do. Then we must *do* it. Only in this way will we be fulfilled.

How do you put the principles we've just discussed to work in your medical practice?

To find out, accompany me down the path once more:

1. *Create a story about your practice.* Your story

should be an idealized version of your medical practice, a vision of what the preeminent Doctor in your field should be—and why. Your story must become the very heart of your practice. It must become the spirit that mobilizes it, as well as everyone who walks through the doors. Without this story, your practice will be reduced to plain work.

2. *Organize your practice so that it breathes life into your story.* Unless your practice can faithfully replicate your story in action, it all becomes fiction. In that case, you'd be better off not telling your story at all. And without a story, you'd be better off leaving your practice the way it is and just hoping for the best.

Here are some tips for organizing your medical practice:

- Identify the key functions of your practice.

- Identify the essential processes that link those functions.

- Identify the results you have determined your practice will produce.

- Clearly state in writing how each phase will work.

Take it step by step. Think of your practice as a program, a piece of software, a system. It is a collaboration, a collection of processes dynamically interacting with one another.

Of course, your practice is also people.

3. *Engage your people in the process*. Why is this the third step rather than the first? Because, contrary to the advice most business experts offer, *you must never engage your people in the process until you yourself are clear about what you intend to do*.

The need for consensus is a disease of today's addled mind, a product of our troubled and confused times. When people don't know what to believe in, they often ask others to tell them. To ask is not to lead but to follow.

The prerequisite of sound leadership is first to know where you wish to go.

And so, "What do *I* want?" becomes the first question; not, "What do *they* want?" In your own practice, the vision must first be yours. To follow another's vision is to abdicate your personal accountability, your leadership role, your true power.

In short, the role of leader cannot be delegated or shared. And without leadership, no medical practice will ever succeed.

Despite what you have been told, *Win-Win* is a *secondary* step, not a primary one. The opposite of *Win-Win* is not necessarily *They Lose*. Let's say "they" can win by choosing a good horse. The best choice will not be made by consensus.

"Guys, what horse do you think we should ride?" will always lead to endless and worthless discussions. By the time you're done jawing, the horse will have already left the post.

Before you talk to your people about what you intend to do in your practice and why you intend to do it, you need to reach agreement with yourself.

It's important to know (1) *exactly* what you want; (2) how you intend to proceed; (3) what's important to you and what isn't; and (4) what you want the practice to be and how you want it to get there.

Once you have that agreement, it's critical that you engage your people in a discussion about what you intend to do and why. Be clear—both with yourself and with them.

THE STORY

The story is paramount because it is your vision. Tell it with passion and conviction. Tell it with precision. Never hurry a great story. Unveil it slowly. Don't mumble or show embarrassment. Never apologize or display false modesty. Look your audience in the eyes and tell your story as though it were the most important one they'll ever hear about business. Your business. The business into which you intend to pour your heart, your soul, your intelligence, your imagination, your time, your money, and your sweaty persistence.

Get into the storytelling zone. Behave as though it means everything to you. Show no equivocation when telling your story.

These tips are important because you're going to tell your story over and over—to patients, to new and old employees, to Doctors and nurses, and to your family and friends. You're going to tell it at work; at your church or synagogue; to your card-playing or fishing buddies; and to organizations such as Kiwanis, Rotary, YMCA, Hadassah, and Boy Scouts.

There are few moments in your life when telling a great story about a great business is inappropriate.

If it is to be persuasive, you must love your story. Do you think Walt Disney loved his Disneyland story? Or Ray Kroc his McDonald's story? What about Dave Smith at Federal Express? Or Debbie Fields at Mrs. Field's Cookies? Or Tom Watson Jr. at IBM?

Do you think these people loved their stories? Do you think others loved (and *still* love) to hear them? I dare say, all successful entrepreneurs have loved the story of their business. Because that's what true entrepreneurs do: They tell stories that come to life in the form of their business.

Remember, a great story never fails. A great story is always a joy to hear.

In summary, you first need to clarify, both for yourself and for your people, the *story* of your practice. Then you need to detail the *process* your practice must go through to make your story become reality. I call this the Business Development Process. Others call it reengineering, continuous improvement, reinventing your practice, or total quality management.

Whatever you call it, you must take three distinct steps to succeed:

1. *Innovation.* Continue to find better ways of doing what you do.

2. *Quantification.* Once that is achieved, quantify the impact of these improvements on your business.

3. *Orchestration.* Once these improvements are verified, orchestrate this better way of running your business so that it becomes your standard, to be repeated time and again.

In this way, the system works no matter who's using it. And you've built a practice that works consistently, predictably, systematically. A practice you can depend on to operate exactly as promised, every single time.

Your vision, your people, your process—all linked.

A superior medical practice is a creation of your imagination, a product of your mind. So fire it up and get started!

I've read that Richard Olivier, son of Sir Laurence, uses Shakespeare's plays to teach leadership and practice skills to executives. I hope he doesn't ignore the scene from *Hamlet* in which Polonius advises Laertes, "To thine own self be true." That is, after all, what we've been talking about in this book.

THE STORY OF DR. HORNBERGER

Dr. Paul W. Hornberger, a Doctor in northern California, realized one day that he wasn't the Doctor he had always pictured in his story. In a piece for the *Santa Rosa Press Democrat,* he explained: "HMOs have decimated the necessary trust between the healer and the sick person. Without trust, healing is not possible. . . . As our forefathers did with an oppressive and greedy British government, doctors (and hospitals) need to declare themselves free from HMOs. Free to give the best health care available."

Aware that self-actualization would forever elude him under the present system, Dr. Hornberger resigned from all HMOs. Other Doctors have joined him. "It has been a risk," he says, "but what was our option?"

But here's the key point: Since his resignation, he's felt rejuvenated. "Several of my colleagues have commented on how much happier I am, that I am excited about being a Doctor again."

Isn't that a goal worth striving for?

For three decades, I've applied The E-Myth principles I've shared here to the successful development of thousands of small businesses throughout the world. Many have been medical practices—from podiatrists to proctologists.

Few rewards are greater than seeing these E-Myth principles improve the work and lives of so many people. Those rewards include seeing these changes:

- Lack of direction—shaped into a path, clearly, lovingly, passionately pursued

- Lack of money or money poorly managed— now understood instead of coveted; created instead of chased; wisely spent or invested instead of squandered

- Lack of committed people—transformed into a cohesive community, working in harmony toward a common goal, discovering each other and themselves in the process, all the while expanding their understanding, their know-how, their interest, their attention

After working with so many Doctors, so many small practitioners, I know that a practice can be much more than what most become. I also know that nothing is preventing you from making your practice all that it can be. It takes only desire and the perseverance to see it through.

Here's the tale of one Doctor who is now happier in his practice and who can envision his hospital operating effectively without him in the future:

THE STORY OF DR. TAYO APAMPA

I run the Korede Hospital in Abeokuta, Ogun State, Nigeria. It was started in 1990 in a building I bought for that purpose. For 12 years before that, I was in a medical partnership. Although it was financially successful, I never felt my dreams were being realized.

In the beginning, we had a motto for the hospital—WE CARE WE SERVE—and a watchword—COURTESY.

We have 12 beds and see 20 to 40 patients daily. We run a daily outpatient clinic 7 days a week, 24-

hour emergency services, and round-the-clock in-patient care. Our focus is family planning and reproductive health, but we attend to a wide range of general illnesses and perform a variety of surgical operations.

I have a staff of 16, including 11 auxiliary nurses, 2 cleaners, a night guard, a driver, and an office assistant. I am considering adding a bookkeeper, an idea I got after reading The E-Myth Revisited.

I am the only Doctor in the hospital, though I occasionally get assistance from local Doctors and visiting consultants. I've tried with varying degrees of success to get experienced Doctors to work with me but finally decided that it would never happen to my satisfaction. When I'm ready to retire, I told myself, I'll just close the practice.

The business has been financially successful, providing me with a relatively comfortable life, but it has taken all my time and alienated me from my children. Until recently, I'd forgotten that the hospital even had a motto or a watchword. I got used to snapping and shouting at my staff to get things done.

After reading The E-Myth Revisited, I discovered that it didn't have to be like that. I suddenly saw clearly my many errors and realized that my dreams could come true.

Now I am attending to the little—but important—things. I conduct regular meetings with senior and junior staff; I am revising my signboard and my logo, all the while gaining a greater understanding *of E-Myth methodologies. I'm happier and can see the hospital running without me in the future.*

I am grateful to Michael for changing my perceptions and giving me a new lease on life and business.

To your practice and your life, good growing!

For more information about how *you* can put The E-Myth to work for you and your business, visit me at:

www.E-Myth.com

and click on . . .

The E-Myth Physician Website.

Or call us at:

1-800-221-0266

and ask for your

FREE TELESEMINAR

**Breaking Free: E-Myth Experience
in Business, Work, and Life.**